Shrinking
History

Shrinking History

On Freud and the Failure of Psychohistory

DAVID E. STANNARD

New York Oxford
OXFORD UNIVERSITY PRESS
1980

Copyright © 1980 by Oxford University Press

Library of Congress Cataloging in Publication Data
Stannard, David E
Shrinking history.

Includes index.
1. Psychohistory. I. Title.
D16.16.S7   901'.9   79-26884   ISBN 0-19-502-735-3

Printed in the United States of America

For Valerie

Contents

Preface   ix
Acknowledgements   xix

The Lessons of Leonardo   1
The Problem of Therapy   31
The Problem of Logic   51
The Problem of Theory   83
The Problem of Culture   117
The Failure of Psychohistory   145

Notes   157
Index   183

Am I obliged to believe *every* absurdity?
And if not, why this one in particular?
There is no appeal to a court above that of reason.

—Sigmund Freud,
The Future of an Illusion

Preface

IN 1958 the French anthropologist Claude Lévi-Strauss observed that the principal difference between history and anthropology can be seen "in their choice of complementary perspectives: History organizes its data in relation to conscious expressions of social life, while anthropology proceeds by examining its unconscious foundations."[1]

In that same year, halfway around the world, there appeared in print the first clear sign that established academic historians would soon begin to reject this apparent truism. In what he called "the next assignment," the president of the American Historical Association exhorted the membership of that organization to get on with the task of examining and analyzing the unconscious foundations of the social life of the past.[2] Such an effort, William L. Langer thought, was long overdue. Magnanimously (though only tentatively) ruling out "constitutional obscurantism" as the source of previous historians' reticence in adopting psychoanalysis, the tool that could unlock the door to the unconscious world of the past, Langer preferred to think that such caution derived merely from a fear of the effects the "coldly penetrating calculus" of psychoanalysis might have on the humanistic tradition of historical explanation. Some unconvinced historians (those, Langer would have said, who remained "buried in their own conservatism") may have preferred to blame their alleged timidity on the constitutional and semantic obscurantism—to use the second meaning of that word—of psychoanalysis.

But no matter. History, at least in the United States, has not been the same since then. A few years after Langer's ringing declaration that the practice of history writing was "on the threshold of a new era," another distinguished member of the profession, in a flush of enthusiasm, went so far as to advocate individual psychoanalysis as part of the professional training of the budding academic historian. While recognizing that "a full psychoanalysis" might not always be necessary or even possible, H. Stuart Hughes wrote that in many cases "it might be precisely what was called for, and I trust that foundation funds would be forthcoming to finance such a venture." He went on:

> I hope that in the coming years a significant minority of young historians, particularly those most concerned with the psychological aspects of historical interpretation, will be going through personal analysis under the guidance of experienced clinicians. For the others, it may be possible to work out a shorter program in consultation with the Psychoanalytic Institutes established near some of our major universities.[3]

As of yet Hughes's hope has not been realized. At least analysis has not commonly become a formal part of graduate school curricula in history. Nevertheless, there remain rather few historical figures of consequence who have not, during the past two decades, been the subject of what self-professed psychohistorian Fawn M. Brodie has referred to as the "surgical operation" of psychohistory.[4] Hardly a professional association meeting passes without a minimum of a session or two on the latest developments in psychohistorical procedure. And there are now at least two scholarly journals extant whose sole purpose is the propagation and examination of psychohistorical analyses.[5]

The quality of this work ranges from the elegant and sensitive writings of Erik H. Erikson, to the tawdry and crackpot disquisitions of too many to name without fear of overlooking others equally deserving of mention. But one example can give at least the flavor of the approach of this latter group.

Writing of the sources behind a "moment of discovery" in his thinking on the psychoanalytic meaning of war, Lloyd de Mause, the founder and editor of *The Journal of Psychohistory*, admits that "technical training" in history and psychoanalysis were of some value to him (although he has no "technical training" in history) because he "had to know how to get around in the literature of both fields." However, he continues:

> Far more crucial were . . . the long hours somewhere around the seventh or eighth year of my personal psychoanalysis when I struggled to re-experience and find meaning in dreams of drowning and sinking in a whirlpool of quicksand, or, when my son was two years old, those hundreds of hours I spent with him pretending we were babies in mommy's belly, crawling around in the dark under the bedclothes and pretending to fall off the bed crying "Help! Save me!," because that was the endless game that seemed to give him a strong sense of the pleasure of mastery.[6]

It was thanks to this sort of thing that de Mause made the inspired discovery that war is nothing less than a reenactment of the experience of birth. The real breakthrough, however, came when he found that military bands beat at the same rate as does "the elevated heart-beat of a woman during a contraction in labor." Thus, de Mause came to understand why he, "a radical and anti-nationalist, was nevertheless moved almost to tears when I stood with my son watching a parade with marching bands . . . . I obviously was a baby being born while watching the parade, being picked up and carried along by my mother's heart-beat whether I felt like it or not, and the tears in my eyes were for the impending separation from my mother!"[7]

If this were representative of the bulk of work being done by psychohistorians it would hardly be necessary to write a book on the subject. Clearly, Mr. de Mause works well beyond the fringe of even the most generous definition of the world of scholarship as do others of his colleagues, such as one Henry Ebel, who "surrounds himself with his historical materials and 'Primals' for hours while free-associating to the material in front of him, in a concentrated effort to reach deeper levels of motivation than the usual reading reveals."[8] (The published results of such "concentrated efforts" can, as one might expect, be rather mind-boggling—e.g., "Bosch, of course, is just a more finicky da Vinci. And da Vinci is just Luther with a talent for sketching.") It is not surprising that de Mause's recent declaration of independence from the discipline of history was greeted with quiet sighs of relief by other, less eccentric, practitioners of the psychohistorical craft—those who do not spend "hundreds of hours" crawling under the bedclothes with a two-year old searching for answers to the riddles of history.[9]

Yet, we must be careful here. For, as often happens when fanatics enter an already questionable field of endeavor, by the very ludicrousness of their positions they may make the work of other, more moderate, participants appear to be models of responsibility. This book argues that this should not be permitted to be the case with psychohistory. While certainly some works of psychohistory are vastly superior to others, little, if any, psychohistory is good history.

This is the conclusion of many (probably most) professional historians. Their reasons for rejecting psychohistory, however, have often not been heard by the general public, nor found convincing by other restless and methodologically inquisitive historians who have of late been seeking out new ways of viewing and interpreting the raw data of the past. It is insufficient, for example, simply to look with disdain upon the poor taste of those who would besmirch the dignity of traditional historical explanation; and to lump psychohistory, as some have done, with the equally new efforts of historians to seek clarification through quantification utterly distorts matters. Moreover, it does not help much to argue, however correctly, that psychohistory attenuates responsibility in history, "trivializes human action. . . . exculpates the vicious and . . . debunks the virtuous"—that is, that it reduces conscious ethical decision-making by such diverse historical figures as Luther, Hitler, Jefferson, Stalin, Gandhi, and others to a crudely mechanistic determinism rooted in ideas concerning the psychopathology of everyday life.[10]

To begin with, history cannot any longer be viewed as Clio, fair maiden among the muses, who must be maintained in the vale, as Jacques Barzun has said, *"virgo intacta."*[11] To adopt or maintain this attitude in response to the challenge of psychohistory is merely to repeat the simple-minded rejection of psychoanalysis itself, when it emerged at the turn of the century, as only an exercise in bad taste and a degradation of human nature. To reject quantitative evaluations of historical data in the same sweeping motion is to court genuine obtuseness: there has, of course, been bad work (as well as very good work) done by quantitative historians, and some of them have made embarrassingly grandiose claims for the limited insights and discoveries resulting from their efforts; but there is no methodological or thematic connection between psychohistory and quantitative analysis that justifies treating them as two elements of a single (and singularly troublesome) phenomenon. Nor, finally, does the argument that psychohistory trivializes both thought and action—that it is a dangerous exercise in the historical exculpation of villains and the debunking of heroes—do little more than underline psycho-historical pretentiousness: such, it is contended, is the price that must always be paid for scientific advance.

This book takes a somewhat different critical approach from those noted above, and I should be candid about it. I was for some time interested in the potential of psychoanalytic theory for opening new ways of looking at historical data, and in other writings I have both urged others and engaged myself in various interdisciplinary borrowings in an effort to coax greater meaning from the fragmented materials of history. I am not at all opposed to open (and admitted) speculation in the writing of history. After all, some of the most important historical advances in modern times have derived from the examination and reexamination of what began as bold speculations.

But mere common sense imposes a limit on this sort of thing. We would not, for instance, see much explanatory value in an effort to show that the cause of this or that historical event was traceable to the fact that the main actor in the event was a Scorpio whose governing planet was Mars; nor would the fact that this actor may have had certain specified facial features be regarded as credible evidence of a constitutional or genetic predisposition to act in a particular fashion; nor would we likely concur with an explanation asserting that such and such happened because God was pleased or displeased with the actor in question. The point is obvious: there is not sufficient believable evidence available to indicate with reasonable assurance that any of these explanatory schemes works. It is as simple as that. Divine intervention may or may not be a reality in the everyday affairs of humankind, but modern historians have generally agreed that analyses based on claims of divine intervention do not deserve a place in historical explanations of events. What is required of God must be

required of all would-be explanation systems, including psychoanalysis; that is, evidence.

Historians have not, to date, seemed especially inclined to investigate this matter at much length. They have other work to do and
thus generally treat psychohistorical work on an ad hoc basis
whenever a particular effort intrudes on their individual fields of
specialization. This book, however, is devoted to precisely that question of theoretical efficacy, to the task of examining what evidence
exists to support various psychoanalytic hypotheses *and* their applicability to history. It is not, apart from a look at a model of sorts in
the first chapter, a critical survey of works thus far written in the field
of psychohistory; for to do that would be to avoid the central question:
does psychoanalytic theory work—does it even make sense?

We will thus be taking up a challenge laid down by Freud more
than half a century ago. In his "Autobiographical Study" of 1925,
Freud claimed that many of his critics had unfairly rejected his work
by "the classical maneuver of not looking through the microscope
so as to avoid seeing what they had denied."[12] Now, there are microscopes and there are microscopes. The one Freud had in mind was his
own: a deep immersion in analysis. Whatever its benefits, such a
procedure hardly deserves to be called looking through a microscope.
A microscope is, after all, a scientific instrument, a piece of equip-
ment—not a conversion experience. To follow Freud's advice on this
matter (and the subsequent advice of legions of defensive analysts) is
much closer to following the suggestion that only those who have
spent an extended period of time as novices among the Jesuits can
properly understand, criticize, or recognize the truth value of the
teachings of Ignatius Loyola. Such an experience might help in
understanding the matters at issue. It might also (more probably) so
distort the individual's perspective that it would *hinder* objective
understanding. In any case, it is hardly intellectually obligatory.

There is a better microscope—the same one to which other systems of explanation must submit. It is the process of simply putting

such systems through some elementary tests designed to determine if they are logically sound, empirically confirmable, and capable of a reasonable degree of generalization. By and large, psychoanalysts have shunned this microscope. Their reasons have been various, but one of the most common, ingenious (and fatuous) is to claim that psychoanalytic theory is so subtle, so complex, and so sophisticated that none of the tools of evaluation yet devised by the best of human minds is capable of testing it.[13] This, like the other common *ad hominem* complaint that critics of psychoanalysis are only displaying their neuroses,[14] is a reply worthy of a mystic or an intellectual charlatan but not someone who wishes to have his or her ideas taken seriously. Because it is so common a claim, however, I will discuss it later at somewhat greater length.

*   *   *

This book, it should be said, is in design something of a primer— a book of elementary principles. In the present case the principles I am concerned with are, as I have said, those having to do with the philosophic, scientific, and universalistic status and validity of psychoanalytic theory. In approaching these matters, I have confined myself largely to the examination of fairly orthodox Freudian theory. In this regard I have allowed myself to be guided by the working psychohistorian. For, despite occasional theoretical forays into the hypothetical world of what psychohistory *might* be, in practice the rule of virtually all writers has been to hew closely to the Freudian line. And even the apparent exceptions—the works of those who rely upon or imitate the ideas of Erik Erikson, for example—remain sufficiently derivative of the Freudian model (in Erikson's own words, "Freud's monumental work is the rock on which such exploration and advancement must be based")[15] that the shape of the discussion that follows is as applicable to that work as it is to Freud's. Moreover, despite all the imaginative so-called alternatives to relatively mainline psychoanalytic theory, *only* fairly orthodox approaches have thus far generated *any* empirical support—and thus, at least insofar as such support is concerned, Freudian theory provides the strongest case *for* the validity of psychohistorical analysis. Other approaches, from the fairy tale world of Lloyd de Mause to the more serious and responsible efforts of such writers as Fred Weinstein and Gerald M. Platt, suffer a single common problem: empirically speaking, they are pipedreams.[16]

Freudian theory (and that of at least the seminal work of the so-called "post-Freudians"—from Jung, Adler, Rank and the other "early schismatics," to Sullivan, Fromm, Horney, Erikson and others) is, of course, generically a therapeutic technique—however much it may subsequently have worked itself into a would-be holistic theory of human behavior of interest to certain social scientists, historians, and students of literature. As a therapeutic technique it requires the existence of a living subject, one willing and able to actively participate in the effort to reach awareness of the allegedly repressed impulses or forgotten traumatic events (and their unique interpretations) that are said to underlie the symptoms in question. This active participation—necessarily involving, it is claimed, transference of intense feelings onto the person of the analyst—is essential to the cooperative process of gaining insight, overcoming resistances, "making the unconscious conscious," and eventually effecting cure.[17] The fact that this is patently and by simple definition impossible when dealing with the scattered literary remains of a long-dead (and therefore, needless to say, inactive and non-participating) subject has led many—most notably a good many psychoanalytically trained clinicians—to dismiss out of hand as what Freud himself called "wild" psychoanalysis the retrospective psychoanalyzing that is the heart of psychohistory.[18] Despite the apparently eminent reasonableness of this rejecting attitude, *from the psychoanalytic perspective itself*, there remains in the minds of many the belief that abstract psychoanalytic *theory* can be applied to historical documents as a method of opening up for scrutiny and intelligent analysis the un-concious mind of the past. Thus, this book—an examination of that theory and its implications for historical analysis.

There is, finally, one more thing that should be said about the presentation of this book as a primer. A primer, ideally, should be written in such a way that it is accessible to the general reader and presents in compact form the essential aspects of an otherwise for-biddingly long, complex, and esoteric argument. My purpose in writing this book in such a way is a simple one: it is merely to help open a long overdue discussion among intelligent laypeople and students of history that has for too long been rendered impossible by the protective smokescreen of functionless private jargon and cant and dogmatic Alice-in-Wonderland logic that has marked the psy-choanalytic and psychohistorical enterprises—a discussion, quite simply, about one small but important aspect of the nature of histor-ical explanation.

Acknowledgments

MOST of the work on this book was carried out in the libraries of Yale and Stanford Universities and the University of California at Santa Cruz. Special thanks are due the staff of the Medical School Library at Yale.

In their earliest stages some of the ideas contained in this book evolved from conversations with Donald M. Lowe, Bruce Kuklick, and David Brion Davis. Drafts of the entire manuscript benefitted from the keen criticisms of William A. Clebsch, Elizabeth A. Davis, Edmund S. Morgan, and two colleagues with serious professional interests in psychohistory, Kai T. Erikson and Joel Bernard.

Daphne Y.F. Chu contributed significantly in a number of ways to the completion of the manuscript; and, although she has not seen the completed work, Valerie M. Stannard endured and contributed much when I was working up a first draft—and thus the book is dedicated to her.

A special note is due Susan Rabiner, the sort of editor every author should have. Since I neglected to thank her in my last book, I would like to do so doubly this time: in ways far beyond what any writer normally expects she has vigorously supported and criticized my work, and in the process has become a valued and trusted friend.

Finally, I should like to acknowledge the work of someone whose name I do not know: the person who gave the title "Shrinking History" to an essay by Robert Coles in *The New York Review of Books*—a title which I have shamelessly stolen for this book.

1

Glendower: I can call spirits from the vasty deep.
Hotspur: Why, so can I, or so can any man;
            But will they come when you do call for
            them?

—William Shakespeare,
*The First Part of King
Henry the Fourth*

The Lessons
of Leonardo

FREUD'S *Leonardo da Vinci and a Memory of His Child-hood*, published in 1910, was the first true example of psychohistori-cal analysis.[1] A genuine *tour de force*, it remains, along with Erik H. Erikson's work, among the finest indicators of the potentials—and the limits—of psychohistory. Within its brief compass this work contains some of the brightest examples of what makes the best psy-chohistory so stimulating: insight, learning, sensitivity, and, most of all, imagination. It also contains some of the clearest illustrations of the pitfalls of works of this sort: it is dazzlingly dismissive of the most elementary canons of evidence, logic, and, most of all, imagin-ative restraint. As one enthusiast has recently written, it is truly "a model for all later psychobiographies."[2] There is much to be learned from it.

Freud begins his study with a brief apology for his intended inva-sion of the privacy of such a great personage as Leonardo, then launches immediately into a search for those most intriguing and possibly revelatory attributes of the great man. Leonardo was known to have possessed what Freud calls a "feminine delicacy of feeling" (exhibited, for instance, in his vegetarianism and his habit of buying caged birds in the market, only to set them free), but was also capable of seemingly contradictory behavior such as studying and sketching the faces of condemned and soon-to-be executed criminals and designing "the cruellest offensive weapons" of war. Leonardo often seemed inactive and indifferent to competition and controversy; he had a habit of leaving work unfinished; he worked very slowly. The list goes on, but initially what interests Freud most is the fact that Leonardo seemed to combine in his adult life a "frigidity," a "cool repudiation of sexuality," and a "stunted" sexual life (evident not only in his behavior but also in his art) with an "insatiable and indefatigable thirst for knowledge."

This last combination of traits is not surprising to Freud. It is, he says, a result of sublimation. "When the period of infantile sexual researches has been terminated by a wave of energetic sexual repression," he asserts, "the instinct for research has three distinct possible vicissitudes open to it owing to its early connection with sexual interests." These are: 1) an inhibition of curiosity; 2) a return of the curiosity in the form of "compulsive brooding," wherein "investigation becomes a sexual activity, often the exclusive one . . . but the interminable character of the child's researches is also repeated in the fact that this brooding never ends and that the intellectual feeling, so much desired, of having found a solution recedes more and more into the distance"; or 3) "in virtue of a special disposition" in some people the investigative impulse provides an outlet for repressed sexuality (the process of sublimation) and "the instinct can operate freely in the service of intellectual interest . . . [while] it avoids any concern with sexual themes."

Leonardo, Freud suggests, seems "a model instance of our third type." But here we encounter difficulty. To substantiate this hypothesis we would "need some picture of his mental development in the first years of his childhood." And there is almost no such information extant. Indeed, Freud admits, all we know of Leonardo's childhood is that he was born in 1452, the illegitimate child of Ser Piero da Vinci, a notary, and "a certain Caterina, probably a peasant girl." Beyond this, the only record of his youth is a 1547 tax register in which the five year old Leonardo is mentioned as a member of Ser Piero's household.

At this point Freud turns to the life of Leonardo from another direction. He quotes a curious passage that appears as an interruption in one of his scientific notes on the flight of birds:

> It seems that I was always destined to be so deeply concerned with vultures; for I recall as one of my very earliest memories, that while I was in my cradle a vulture came down to me, and opened my mouth with its tail, and struck me many times with its tail against my lips.

So important does Freud find this sentence that he announces his intent to use it, by means of "the techniques of psycho-analysis," to "fill the gap in Leonardo's life story by analyzing his childhood fantasy." The analysis that follows is nothing short of imaginative wizardry.

The tail of the vulture, beating against Leonardo's infant lips, is translated into a "substitutive expression" for a penis. The scene is thus illustrative of fellatio, of a "passive" homosexual experience. But there is another side to the fantasy, Freud notes, since the desire to suck on a penis "may be traced to an origin of the most innocent kind": "merely a reminiscence of sucking—or being suckled—at his mother's breast."

But why is the bird a vulture? At this point Freud's great breadth of learning takes over: in ancient Egyptian hieroglyphics "the mother is represented by a picture of a vulture." Further, the name of a vulture-like Egyptian female deity was pronounced *mut*—a sound very similar to *Mutter* (mother). In addition, other classical writings indicate that "the vulture was regarded as a symbol of motherhood because only female vultures were believed to exist"—females who conceive "in mid-flight" when they "open their vaginas and are impregnated by the wind," a notion used by certain Fathers of the Church "as a proof drawn from natural history" against those who doubted the virgin birth and a notion with which, Freud writes, "it can hardly be doubted" Leonardo was aware. The importance of the vulture fantasy to Leonardo, then, can be seen in his recognition "that he also had been such a vulture-child—he had had a mother, but no father. . . . [and] in this way he was able to identify himself with the child Christ, the comforter and savior not of this one woman alone."

Having so ingeniously solved the puzzle of Leonardo's vulture fantasy, Freud returns to the problem of the lack of information available on Leonardo's childhood beyond the date of his birth and his parentage and the lonely fact that he appears as a member of his father's household at age five. Freud writes that since "the replacement of his mother by the vulture indicates that the child was aware of his father's absence and found himself alone with his mother," the vulture fantasy serves as a replacement for the missing historical data as it "seems to tell us" that Leonardo spent "the first critical years of his life not by the side of his father and stepmother, but with his poor, forsaken, real mother, so that he had time to feel the absence of his father."

Freud thenceforth accepts this surmise as "this fact about his childhood" and determines that Leonardo's having "spent the first years of his life alone with his mother, will have been of decisive influence in the formation of his inner life." How decisive? So decisive that Leonardo, "more than other children," would have encountered the problem of the missing father. The fact that he would "brood on this riddle with special intensity," indeed that he was "tormented as he was by the great question of where babies come from and what the father has to do with their origin," thus explains (it was "an inevitable effect of this state of affairs," Freud says) why Leonardo "at a tender age became a researcher."

Content now with his reconstruction of Leonardo's outer and inner lives during his infancy and early childhood, Freud next turns to the problem of connecting these analytically unearthed childhood experiences with Leonardo's adult behavior and predispositions. He begins again with the vulture: how is it possible, Freud asks, that this maternal image is furnished with a symbol of maleness—a tail which "cannot possibly signify anything other than a male genital, a penis." For an answer Freud draws on his then-developing theory of infantile sexuality.

The young male child, Freud believed, always assumes that everyone (including his mother) has a penis. Even when confronted with evidence to the contrary, the child assumes that the female once had a penis, but that it was cut off. Since all this thinking derives initially from the child's great interest in his own genitals he then becomes threatened by the possibility "that the organ which is so dear to him will be taken away from him if he shows his interest in it too plainly. . . . [and] henceforth he will tremble for his masculinity, but at the same time he will despise the unhappy creatures on whom the cruel punishment has, as he supposes, already fallen." A further bit of insight regarding the vulture fantasy now becomes clear to Freud: at the time when Leonardo directed his "fond curiosity" to his mother he still believed her to have a penis. This insight becomes "more evidence of Leonardo's early sexual researches, which in our opinion had a decisive effect on the whole of his later life."

But decisive in what way? It is decisive, Freud observes, in that it allows us to begin seeking "a causal connection between Leonardo's relation with his mother in childhood and his later manifest, if ideal [sublimated], homosexuality."

The pursuit of this "causal connection" starts with Freud's clinical observations that homosexuals have in early life "a very intense erotic attachment to a female person, as a rule their mother." This attachment, though subsequently forgotten, is "evoked or encouraged by too much tenderness on the part of the mother herself, and further reinforced by the small part played by the father during their childhood." (This situation, of course, precisely describes Leonardo's childhood, at least as reconstructed in Freud's analysis of the vulture fantasy.) The erotic attachment to the mother, Freud notes, is eventually repressed by the young male, but only because "he puts himself in her place, identifies himself with her." Such attachments may be avoided by "the presence of a strong father [which] would ensure that the son made the correct decision in his choice of object, namely someone of the opposite sex." In some lives, however, this is not to be the case—and instead the process that leads to self-identification with the mother results in adult homosexuality: "for the boys whom he now loves as he grows up are after all only substitutive figures and revivals of himself in childhood—boys whom he loves in the way in which his mother loved *him* when he was a child."

This analysis of infantile sexuality is critical to the unfolding picture of Leonardo because it provides the theoretical link between the nature of Leonardo's childhood experiences and the "historical probability" that beneath the "cool sexual rejection" that seemed to characterize much of his adult life, there lay the fact that Leonardo was "one who was emotionally homosexual." True, evidence to support this contention is rather thin. Indeed, it is singular and questionable: at age twenty-four Leonardo was anonymously accused, with three others, of homosexuality; the accusation was investigated and the charges were dismissed. That is all. But for Freud it is just the beginning. He then couples with this historical datum the additional information that Leonardo often took as pupils handsome young men toward whom he showed kindness and consideration. (Lest one miss the implications of this fact, Freud goes out of his way to note that in so showing kindness and consideration to his pupils Leonardo was caring for them "just as his own mother might have tended him.") Further, Leonardo's diary contains, among its many entries, notes of small financial expenditures on his pupils. This appears to be innocent enough, but not for the psychoanalyst: "the fact that he left these pieces of evidence" of kindness "calls for explanation."

Freud points out that among Leonardo's papers is also a different note of financial expenditure—one for the funeral of a woman identified only as Caterina, the same name, it must be remembered, as his mother's. Indeed, Freud says (although there is no evidence to substantiate the assertion) that this Caterina *was* Leonardo's mother. When set side by side with the entries regarding expenditures on his pupils, this note for funeral expenditures tells a dramatic and hitherto unknown story: although constrained and inhibited from conscious expression, Leonardo's repressed feelings of erotic attraction for his mother and his pupils take on the character of an "obsessional neurosis" made evident by his "compulsion to note in laborious detail the sums he spent on them." The artist's hidden life now becomes apparent as this wealth of accumulated evidence allows us to see Leonardo's unconscious mind betraying what his conscious mind never could: "It was through this erotic relation with my mother that I became a homosexual."

Finally Freud comes to the relevancy of his analysis for understanding Leonardo's powers of artistic expression. We soon find that this reconstructed sexual biography is responsible for the greatness of Leonardo's *Mona Lisa* and other paintings and that "the key to all his achievements and misfortunes lay hidden in the childhood phantasy of the vulture."

Returning once again to the vulture/mother fantasy, Freud notes that it "is compounded from the memory of being suckled and being kissed by his mother." In fact, "this may be translated," Freud writes, thusly: "My mother pressed innumerable passionate kisses on my mouth."

With that translation in mind, Freud turns to one of the outstanding characteristics of Leonardo's later paintings: "the remarkable smile, at once fascinating and puzzling, which he conjured up on the lips of his female subjects." It seems that, in encountering on the face of his model for the *Mona Lisa* this "smile of bliss and rapture" something was awakened in Leonardo "which had for long lain dormant in his mind—probably an old memory." It was, of course, the memory of his mother and the smile that had once encircled her mouth. Although by this time "he had long been under the dominance of an inhibition which forbade him ever again to desire such caresses from the lips of women," he could and did thenceforth endeavor "to reproduce the smile with his brush, giving it to all his pictures."

Such subsequent pictures include, most notably for Freud, the famous *Anna Metterza* which depicts the child Jesus, his mother Mary, and her mother Saint Anne. The faces of both women, Freud notes, contain smiles similar to that on the *Mona Lisa*, though the "uncanny and mysterious character" of the original is now replaced by "inward feeling and quiet blissfulness." In addition, there is something at least equally striking: Saint Anne is depicted as possessed of an unfaded beauty making her appear generationally coterminous with her daughter Mary. The conclusion is inescapable. This painting, says Freud, contains nothing less than "the synthesis of the history of his [Leonardo's] childhood." Freud had shown, earlier, through his analysis of the vulture fantasy, how Leonardo identified himself with the Christ child. Now he shows how this identification is represented in Leonardo's art which gives the Christ child two mothers, just as Leonardo himself had two mothers— Caterina and his "kind stepmother, Donna Albiera." Leonardo endows each of the mothers with the maternal smile of his own childhood memory, the memory that had returned to him when he had reencountered the smile on the model for his *Mona Lisa.** From this point on the paintings of Leonardo often seem marked by this enigmatic smile, and thus "with the help of the oldest of all his erotic impulses he enjoyed the triumph of once more conquering the inhibition in his art."

There is much more in Freud's biography that might be treated here, including the analysis of a slight error (for some reason only one of several is singled out) in Leonardo's recording of the death of his father. Freud uses this analysis to explain the artist's failure to finish paintings as well as his independence of mind. But enough has already been seen to understand the general shape and method of the argument.

*   *   *

It is difficult to know exactly where to begin in evaluating this work. Even a historically untrained person with little knowledge of Leonardo's life, unless extraordinarily gullible and naïvely convinced of the magical powers of psychoanalysis, would have *some* questions to ask concerning the logical and evidentiary leaps and bounds Freud makes.

But let us begin with what Freud considered the pivotal event in his analysis—the vulture fantasy. There was no vulture fantasy. The only time in his extant writings that Leonardo even mentions a vulture is under the heading "Gluttony" in that section of *The Note-*

---

* In a later edition of this work Freud added at this point his tentative approval (complete with illustration) of a "remarkable discovery" by his disciple Oskar Pfister that the *Anna Metterza* contains—cleverly concealed in "the curiously arranged and rather confusing drapery" of Mary's robe—"the *outline of a vulture*" with its tail leading directly to the Christ child's lips. Pfister was not alone in conducting this sort of detective work. There have been others, from C. G. Jung who, prior to Pfister, found a vulture lurking somewhere else in the painting, to Raymond Stites who claims to have found several fetuses, in varying stages of development, beneath St. Anne's right foot.[3]

books that is entitled "A Bestiary." The reference reads, in its entirety: "The vulture is so given up to gluttony that it would go a thousand miles in order to feed on carrion, and this is why it follows armies." Now this statement, I think it fair to say, does not lend much support to Freud's thesis that Leonardo unconsciously associated the image of the vulture with his beloved mother, thus recognized "that he also had been such a vulture-child," and by extension was led "to identify himself with the child Christ." On the contrary, the entry suggests that Leonardo had a rather different image of the vulture than the virgin-mother of the Church Fathers—the image of which Freud had asserted, "it can hardly be doubted" Leonardo was aware.

But what about that recollection of an early memory? It does exist, written on the back of a page that contains various notations on the flight of birds (a subject which, along with anatomy, weight, and the nature of water, he seems to have found particularly interesting); but the creature in question is a kite, a small hawk-like bird. It was a kite, not a vulture, that Leonardo recalled opening his mouth and striking his lips with its tail. The kite, of all the birds he wrote about, seems to have been of most interest to Leonardo, but the only time he imbues it with qualities that might be of interest to the psychobiographer is in the same "bestiary" section of *The Notebooks* in which he also mentions the vulture. The reference is under the heading "Envy" and is cold comfort to would-be supporters of Freud's thesis. "Of the kite," it says, "one reads that when it sees that its children in the nest are too fat it pecks their sides out of envy and keeps them without food."

It must be said, in Freud's defense, that this crucial error was really not his fault. For his information on Leonardo Freud seems to have relied heavily on D. S. Merezhkovsky's 1895 biography which contains, in its German translation, a mistranslation that substitutes "vulture" for "kite." The error was pointed out as early as 1923, but does not seem to have much troubled subsequent psychoanalytic evaluators of the work, despite Freud's own assertion that the vulture fantasy was "the key" to all Leonardo's "achievements and misfortunes."[4] James Strachey, general editor of *The Standard Edition of the Complete Psychological Works of Sigmund Freud*, did refer to the error once, in a personal communication with Ernest Jones, as "an awkward fact." In his "Editor's Note" to *The Standard Edition's* version of the Leonardo book, however, Strachey dismisses the error as but "one piece of corroborative support" for the "psychological analysis of the phantasy" and claims that "the main body of Freud's study is unaffected by his mistake." Jones also considers the error to be "this unessential part of Freud's argument," as does Kurt R. Eissler who writes that the resulting problem affects not "the kind of conclusion that Freud drew but only . . . the particular premise on which the conclusion rested" and thus, he goes on to say, "in so far as Freud's interpretation does not refer specifically to the kind of bird, it may be expected to be correct." (These are words that deserve careful re-reading.) Similarly, and perhaps most recently, Joseph D. Lichtenberg insists that, while admittedly "unfortunate," the mistake "affects only the weight of confirmatory evidence for Freud's interpretation of the meaning of the childhood memory—not the hypothesis itself."[5]

These are brave, but misguided, rescue efforts. To put it simply: Freud built most of his analysis in the manner of an inverted pyramid, the whole structure balancing on the keystone of a single questionable fact and its interpretation; once that fact is shown to be wrong, and removed as support, the entire edifice begins to crumble. And no amount of rhetorical waffling or smoke screening can conceal that process of natural disintegration.

To begin with, the entire body of contingent hypotheses that Freud joined to the vulture fantasy (hypotheses that themselves, in his hands, soon became "facts") now lose relevance. Since there was no vulture in the avian fantasy (and since the only evidence we have of Leonardo's attitude toward the *kite* suggests a very different range of symbolic meanings—if any—for that imagined experience) we no longer have *any* reason to believe that Leonardo was aware of or concerned (consciously or unconsciously) by his father's alleged absence during his childhood—the analysis of the specific *vulture* symbolism having been the *sole* initiating source of this idea. Further, since Freud relied entirely on his analysis of the vulture fantasy to "fill the gap" in Leonardo's childhood history, we now no longer have *any* reason to believe that Leonardo in fact *did* spend those years alone with his mother. Indeed, evidence unearthed subsequent to Freud's work now indicates quite strongly that the contrary was the case, that Leonardo was a welcomed member of his father's household from the time of his birth.[6]

The contrived facts of Leonardo's childhood, now suddenly gone from the story, are, however crucial, just the first part of the problem. They are important to Freud only insofar as he can link them with other matters—this time, certain facts of Leonardo's adult life. As with his childhood, these facts (at least those of interest to Freud, that is, those suggestive of homosexuality) are precious few and very chancy. First, there is the anonymous accusation leveled at four young men in 1476, one of whom happened to be Leonardo, that was officially examined at the time and *dismissed*. Freud himself admits this accusation probably occurred in the first place only "because he [Leonardo] had employed a boy of bad reputation as a model." One may wonder why Freud is so ready to discount evidence he himself has just introduced. It may be (one can only conjecture here) because the accusation of active homosexuality is not really necessary to his argument. (Indeed, it is actually detrimental to it, since that argument depends on the conviction that Leonardo's alleged homosexuality was not active but was *sublimated*.) Why then introduce the matter at all? Perhaps for tactical reasons—few other explanations make sense. For by bringing the accusation to the reader's attention, but then leaving it in a questionable and unresolved state, Freud creates enough doubt to at least lend credibility to an otherwise *wholly imaginary* assertion: that Leonardo's sexual interests, sublimated or not, were in fact homosexual. From that point on, this one specious conjecture serves to focus all the discrete fragments of evidence Freud has unearthed: 1) the childhood history that has been constructed for Leonardo (one that Freud's clinical experience—though involving, he admits, only "a small number of persons"—finds as common among adult homosexuals); 2) the accusation of homosexuality as a young man; 3) the many small kindnesses Leonardo showed to his pupils (most of whom were—as of course *all* artists, craftsmen, or teachers of any sort were at that time—young males) and recorded in his diary; 4) the recorded note of expenditures for the funeral of one "Caterina," whom Freud takes to be Leonardo's mother; 5) the lack of evidence that Leonardo had an adult sex life of any kind; and 6) Leonardo's insatiable desire to investigate the world about him.

For Freud, the conclusion seems inescapable: Leonardo became homosexual as a result of his early childhood experience, but by the process of sublimation his sexuality found expression in a relentless quest for knowledge; only in his unconsciously motivated "compulsion to note in laborious detail the sums he spent on them" did he betray the fact that his mother and his pupils "had been his sexual objects." We must examine this argument in steps.

1) We now know that there is *no* evidence to support the idea that Leonardo's early childhood was as Freud surmised—that is, that it paralleled that of the unspecified "small number" of homosexuals of Freud's clinical experience. In fact, the evidence we do have supports the very opposite conclusion. But even if Freud *had* been correct in his historical reconstruction, the most large-scale and sophisticated modern studies of the genesis of homosexuality provide no support for either the alleged importance of castration anxiety or for the importance of the Freudian warm mother/distant father hypoth-

esis.[7] In sum: Freud's reconstruction of Leonardo's early childhood must be discarded as historically worthless and clinically not much better.

2) Leonardo was *acquitted* of the allegation of homosexuality and there is no other historically acceptable evidence of homosexuality. Even if there *were* support for this contention it would not help Freud's case, which is based on Leonardo's presumed *sublimation* of his sexual impulses. In sum: the question of Leonardo's active homosexuality must be discarded as historically worthless, and in any case irrelevant to Freud's own argument.

3) This bit of evidence seems correct, though *by itself* utterly trivial: Leonardo did keep a record of money spent on his pupils.

4) Leonardo did record an expenditure for the funeral of a woman named Caterina. There is no reason, however, to believe that this Caterina was his mother, while there *is* reason to believe she was his house servant of the same name, the same apparent house servant named Caterina who appears in Leonardo's financial accounts twice earlier as the recipient of "ten soldi" payments.[8] (It is also worthy of at least passing note that, while Leonardo does not further identify Caterina, when he records the death of his father Leonardo explicitly identifies him as "Ser Piero da Vinci, my poor father!") In sum: Freud's assumption that this Caterina was Leonardo's mother must be discarded as historically unestablished and most probably quite wrong. Further, if, as seems probable, this Caterina was not Leonardo's mother, then the expenditures on her funeral become irrelevant to Freud's argument.[9]

5) It is true that there is no evidence that suggests an active adult sex life for Leonardo, though negative evidence of this sort must be treated with a good deal of caution. There is also no evidence to indicate that Leonardo washed behind his ears, masturbated, or came in out of the rain, but lack of evidence cannot be taken as proof that he did *not* do these things. That the problem here is a common one among historians does not make it less serious.[10] In sum: the

possibility that Leonardo may have been sexually inactive *may* be taken as of some *very low level* biographical interest *if* a significant number of historically credible and related facts make such a conjecture relevant. In Freud's work, at least, such facts do not exist. Thus, this matter too must be discarded.

6) This assertion is indeed correct: like most, probably all, great scientists and artists Leonardo did have a deep interest in investigation.

Thus far, then, after discarding those of Freud's notions that are flatly incorrect, unsupportable, and/or irrelevant, we are left with the following: Leonardo left no record of sexual activity of any sort; he kept a record of small expenditures, some of which concerned his pupils; he was also very curious about things. That is all.

We turn now to the truly exciting part of Freud's biography, in which he links his analysis of Leonardo's life with the character of his art. The main foci here are two: 1) the "smile of bliss and rapture" on the face of the *Mona Lisa* (believed by many to have been the wife of the Florentine, Francesco del Giocondo) and subsequently a similar smile on the faces of Saint Anne and Mary in the *Anna Metterza*, as well as on such later figures as John the Baptist and Leda; and 2) the generationally coterminous appearance, in the *Anna Metterza*, of Anne and Mary, despite the fact that they were mother and daughter.* (Of course, by this time Freud's thesis, based on the assumption that Leonardo was unconsciously motivated by specific early childhood experiences, makes no sense at all. Still, it is instructive to look independently at this concluding section of the argument.)

It is crucial to Freud that the famed "Leonardesque" smile first appears on the *Mona Lisa* and only later in other of his works. For it was the woman depicted in that painting, he says, who reawakened

---

*For obvious reasons I will not here belabor the embarrassing matter of the "hidden vulture" in the folds of Mary's robe.

in Leonardo the "old memory" of his mother's smile which had "long lain dormant in his mind." The problem now, then, is an art historical one. Freud is dealing with extremely subtle and subjective nuance here, not only in his characterization of the Mona Lisa smile and in his attribution of similarity between it and the female smiles on the *Anna Metterza*, but also in his necessary claim that nothing quite like it *precedes* the *Mona Lisa*. But since it is well known, as Edward MacCurdy has put it, that no more than about "a dozen pictures are all that can be attributed to Leonardo with any degree of certitude or even probability," and since not all of these portray smiling women, it would seem that Freud has made for himself a virtually irrefutable case.[11] Certainly, at the very least it will be very difficult to find contradictory evidence that is factual rather than subjective and intuitive.

It can be argued, for instance, that those very few works that are attributable to Leonardo include at least one, the *Virgin of the Rocks* (1483), that predates by almost two decades his work on the *Mona Lisa* and that contains female mouths that, if not clear precedents of hers are at least remarkably similar. Perhaps even most of his work can be shown to possess this characteristic, beginning with the mouth on Leonardo's youthful head of an angel in his teacher Verrochio's *Baptism of Christ* and including that of Mary in Leonardo's own first major independent work, the *Adoration of the Kings*. The eminent art historian Meyer Schapiro has also pointed out that Verrochio himself painted "several smiling faces of a subtlety of expression approaching the later pictures of Leonardo," thus suggesting the possibility that, as with other of Leonardo's themes, there was in the smile a derivative element traceable to his teacher's work.[12] In addition, there are other works, of other artists, produced in the same general era that share—at least from a figurative perspective— this characteristic: in sculpture, for example, Rosselino's *Virgin* is so adorned. Beyond this, however, it could be contended that even if the so-called "Leonardesque" smile *did* appear suddenly, and without a hint of precedent, on the face of the *Mona Lisa*, there is not a shred of evidence to support Freud's conjecture that the encounter with his model stirred in Leonardo a childhood memory; there are countless other possible reasons, each with as much evidentiary support as Freud supplies for his own conjecture (that is to say none), that might be suggested as motivation for Leonardo's subsequent use of that expression.

But finally, there *is* one bit of factual evidence that, particularly when added to the above objections, makes Freud's case simply wrong. It is the fact that there exists a preliminary cartoon of the *Anna Metterza* that predates by several years the *Mona Lisa*. And in that cartoon the faces of Saint Anne and Mary possess the very same smiles as in the later full painting, the same painting that Freud incorrectly assumed *followed* the inspiration induced by Mona Lisa.[13] In short, mere chronology is sufficient to show Freud's thesis to be incorrect.

The other major consideration concerning Leonardo's later painting involves the apparent similarity of age on the faces of Saint Anne and Mary in the *Anna Metterza*. This suggested to Freud that Leonardo, who supposedly identified himself with the Christ child, was unconsciously painting, "the synthesis of the history of his childhood" in which he had, Freud thought, two mothers. Although in his analysis of the avian fantasy Freud had keyed Leonardo's Christ child identification to the fact that, like the mythological vulture, his actual mother (like Mary) had no male partner, for some unexplained reason, in his analysis of the *Anna Metterza* Freud argues that Mary is the representation of Leonardo's *stepmother* and Saint Anne is his actual mother. Leonardo, Freud writes, "seems to have used the blissful smile of Saint Anne to disavow and to cloak the envy which the unfortunate woman felt when she was forced to give up her son to her better-born rival, as she had once given up his father as well." Now, apart from this characteristic bit of confusion, this argument is premised on the assumption that by portraying the

two women as near-contemporaries Leonardo was making a new
and unusual artistic statement. In fact, he was not.

As Meyer Schapiro has shown at some length, "contrary to Freud's
belief, Anne and Mary had been represented together as young saints
long before Leonardo."[14] Age similarity was a quite common characteristic of such Holy Family paintings, dating at least from a 1367
work by the Sienese Luca di Tomé (in which Anne is simply a replica
of her daughter, or vice versa) and including the work of such
contemporaries of Leonardo as Dürer and Cranach (an altarpiece of
the latter, in fact, portrays Anne as possibly even younger than
Mary).[15] Freud's failing in this case was simply due to unfamil-
iarity with the artistic and cultural context within which his subject
worked.

And so, at each of the three essential steps in Freud's argument—
the early childhood history, the adult sexual life, and the later painting characteristics—we find virtually no supporting evidence. Each
step *independently* fails to withstand scrutiny, even though, because
of the posited scheme of interlocking causality, all that would really
be necessary to undermine Freud's argument is the fatal criticism of
the very first step, the analysis of the unfortunate vulture fantasy.

Is there, then, nothing to be learned from Freud's study? Of course
there is. Simply by addressing his subject in the bold way that he
did, Freud broke through the crust of hagiography that had so often
characterized previous works on Leonardo and in so doing he raised
a variety of truly new and important *questions* that others might
later pursue in a somewhat more restrained and responsible fashion.
Even Meyer Schapiro, in some ways perhaps the sharpest critic of
this work, concedes that much.

Perhaps, however, the most interesting insights to be gained from
Freud's *Leonardo* concern not Leonardo but Freud himself. For
unlike the story of Leonardo's life, about Freud we know quite a bit.
And much of what we know shows that a good deal of what Freud
claimed to find characteristic of Leonardo was characteristic of him-

self: an insatiable curiosity; a great love for his mother; a strong desire for privacy; extreme sexual repression; a very early withdrawal from all sexual activity; an acknowledged "piece of unruly homosexual feeling" and a "pronounced mental bi-sexuality"; a hesitancy about publishing completed works and a habit of declaring that none of his creations was complete; a rejection of "both dogmatic and personal religion"; and finally a triumph of creativity "at the very summit of his life," to use Freud's own words in describing Leonardo—Freud was in his early fifties when he wrote the Leonardo study, almost precisely the same age at which Leonardo painted the *Mona Lisa*.[16]

This is just the sort of thing that makes for fine moments of armchair musing and psychologizing—and at best perhaps the forming a genuine hypothesis or two—but not much else. The same is true of Freud's *Leonardo*.

* * *

It is, I hope, now obvious that a book examining psychohistory as an intellectual enterprise could not fruitfully be made up merely of a series of critiques such as this. Not only would such an effort never be sufficiently inclusive, but it would also be fruitlessly repetitive and its argument eventually subject to a very simple and correct criticism—that what was wrong with the works under review could be remedied simply by doing *better* psychohistory. It is a premise of this book that the best *possible* psychohistory would still be bad history because of the limitations imposed by the weaknesses of the underlying theoretical structure. This premise, then, is the subject of the rest of this book.

Nevertheless, there were good reasons for beginning with an example such as Freud's. First, since this is something of a primer, Freud's example provides the uninitiated reader with a sample of the type of work done by the psychohistorian. Second, by beginning with Freud's *Leonardo*, this reader is exposed to a sample from the pen of the father of all psychohistorians, and a sample that remains, despite its myriad problems, one of the finest and most restrained such works available. (Subsequent psychoanalyses of Leonardo, for example—from Marie Bonaparte's in 1927 to Kurt Eissler's in 1961—make Freud's work appear positively prosaic.) Third, and most important, in Freud's *Leonardo* we see in brief form the full range of problems that afflict virtually all works of psychohistory, up to and including those of Erik H. Erikson, likely the best of the genre. These problems can be sorted into four general categories: problems of fact; problems of logic; problems of theory; and problems of culture. It is worth a cursory look at them.

Problems of fact is a self-explanatory category. It includes such things as fiction writing to "fill gaps" in the historical record. A well-known example of this, from the work of Erikson, appears in his *Young Man Luther*. As did Freud in his book on Leonardo, Erikson begins his second chapter with a description of a key event in his subject's life: the time when, it is reported, Luther was seated in the choir of the monastery at Erfurt and, upon hearing a reading from the gospel of the exorcism of a deaf and dumb demoniac, fell to the floor "and roared with the voice of a bull"—"I am not!" "I am not!" By so doing, Erikson says, Luther was in effect making the "childlike protestation of somebody who has been called a name or who has been characterized with loathsome adjectives: here, dumb, mute, possessed."

Erikson thinks it would be "interesting to know whether at this moment Martin roared in Latin or in German." It would, in fact, be more interesting to know whether he roared at all. It is probable, considering the quality of the evidence, that he did not. The evidence for the "fit in the choir" incident is a bit of gossip filtered through several levels of hearsay and promoted entirely by outspoken enemies of Luther. For Erikson to repeat the incident and to use it as the key event in the first analytic chapter in his book is, as one theologian notes, "rather like citing seriously and discussing extensively a report about Freud whose only source is a succession of Nazi anti-Semites, and which was published by one of them only in its fourth retelling."[17]

Erickson, it must be acknowledged, recognizes the weakness of the evidence that the fit in the choir ever took place and dutifully refers to it at one point as "this alleged event." But before long it has been integrated fully into his argument and is referred to without qualification; that is, as fact. He even goes so far as to justify its inclusion in his analysis by saying that it does at least have a "ring of truth"; and the fact that Luther himself never mentioned the alleged event may be because "he may well have had an amnesia," another irresponsible passing comment blithely plucked from thin air to shore up an edifice of sheer conjecture.

A similar process occurs in Erikson's description of Luther's father. It is important to Erikson's case that Luther have a malicious and tyrannical father, in order that the young man's harsh image of the "Father in heaven" can be analyzed as a projection of the image of his earthly father. So, Erikson gives Luther a brutal, malicious, and tyrannical father. Again, like Freud, Erikson readily admits that there are almost no facts extant regarding Luther's childhood, but one fact that he asserts is that Luther's parents were "hard, thrifty, and superstitious, and beat their boy." Much is made of this parental oppression and general "maltreatment" of the young boy. But what is the evidence? The evidence consists *entirely* of *two* references, attributed to Luther by others, to beatings received as a child—one delivered by his mother, one by his father—and each reference closes by indicating that the parent either meant well (the mother) or subsequently made an effort to win back the boy's affection (the father). Further, even this negligible evidence of mistreatment is of questionable value since its source is Luther's *Table Talk,* a collection of sayings recorded by his students when he was fifty years old, produced in differing versions and never even seen by Luther. In addition, this flimsy anecdotal evidence runs directly contrary to a comparative wealth of material indicating that a great deal of love and respect obtained within the household of Luther's childhood. It is this sort of loose overstatement in the face of patently contradictory evidence that has led even the most open-minded of authorities on Luther, men such as Roland Bainton and Heinrich Bornkamm, to refer to Erikson's "violent distortions," his "heap of exaggerations and groundless speculations." In both cases these critics were not at all unfriendly to the idea of psychohistory, but were simply insistent that "a pyramid of conjectures" was insufficient grounding for such an effort—as Bainton put it, one must first simply "get the facts straight."[18]

Problems of logic. This category is central to the failings of psychohistory. As with all of these categories, parallels between Freud's *Leonardo* and virtually all subsequent psychohistorical efforts abound. The one (of many) I mention here overlaps with the problem of fact. Not only do Freud, Erikson, and others of much lesser eminence and talent violate basic rules of evidence by inventing numerous facts crucial to their arguments, but in their most common *method* of doing so they breach one of the most fundamental principles of logic. *Post hoc, ergo propter hoc* describes the error built on the assumption that if event *B* followed event *A*, then *B* must have happened *because* of *A*. This is a common enough mistake in all historical writing, but since Freud it has been given a dizzying new twist: it is now apparently no longer necessary to historically establish the *existence* of *A*. So long as *B* is found to exist, it is *assumed* that *A must have* happened since *B* is a psychoanalytically posited *consequence* of *A*. Once having ascertained, then (by means of conjecture), the alleged existence of *A*, the *cause* of *B*'s existence is made clear: it exists because of *A*—even though there may be not a shred of real evidence that *A* ever existed! An example should make this problem more clear.

In his psychohistorical study, *Fathers and Children: Andrew Jackson and the Subjugation of the American Indian,* Michael Paul Rogin encounters the same initial problem encountered by Freud with Leonardo and Erikson with Luther—no information on his subject's early childhood; that is, in the logical sequence, no *A*. Rogin compounds this difficulty by using an analytic approach borrowed from Melanie Klein, an approach that concentrates the crucial personality-shaping influences within the first two years of life and, in fact, places greatest emphasis on the first six months.[19] Rogin knows nothing about this period of Jackson's life, except the fact that Jackson's father died before he was born and that he was raised by his mother in his sister's household. He does, however, know a good deal about Jackson's adult life, ranging from his quick temper to his varied medical problems, which Rogin claims are "commonly" derivative of "tensions in the early maternal tie." Simpler explanations that have at least some evidentiary credibility (such as the quite plausible possibility that mercury poisoning was responsible for some of his medical difficulties) are given short shrift.[20] In no time at all, Kleinian theory, along with bits and pieces of other psychoanalytic ideas (at least one of which is thoroughly misused), has allowed Rogin to explain these and other aspects of Jackson's adult life in terms of his earliest childhood, even though almost nothing is known about that childhood.[21]

This would be reckless enough, it would seem, but Rogin takes his analysis an immense step further, adding still more to the logical muddle. Arguing that "a great man embodies in extreme form the central cultural tensions of his time" (certainly itself a dubious assumption) and that "Jackson was no ordinary President" (without telling us who, in contrast, *was* an "ordinary President"), Rogin claims that through Jackson's psychological biography we can view, writ small, nothing less than the psychological biography of antebellum America. After all, Rogin asserts, "to pick Jackson to represent ante-bellum America . . . is to make the same choice as his contemporaries." By this logic, every President (except, for some reason, those who can be deemed "ordinary") can be seen, since they were elected by their contemporaries, as being the psychic embodiments of their times. This kind of historical and psychological naïveté has not been seen among "ordinary" historians for decades. In purely logical terms, however, it is reminiscent of the story told by David Hackett Fischer in his discussion of "the fallacy of the lonely fact":

> There is a story, perhaps apocryphal, of a scientist who published an astonishing and improbable generalization about the behavior of rats. An incredulous colleague came to his laboratory and politely asked to see the records of the experiments on which the generalization was based. "Here they are," said the scientist, dragging a notebook from a pile of papers on his desk. And pointing to a cage in the corner, he added, "there's the rat."[22]

At least with the rat there is a good chance that something is known about his (or her) childhood.

Problems of theory. This problem involves the *method* that the psychohistorian uses to invent the facts of a subject's childhood before showing those facts to be the causes of adult behavior. One can read through stacks of psychohistorical writings without ever encountering evidence that the authors did anything but take psychoanalytic theory as a scientific given—as Freud put it, "the key" to understanding action. If psychoanalytic theory is such a key, then at least some of the weakness inherent in the problems of fact and logic might be dissipated. But it is not. In Freud's *Leonardo* I have already pointed out that much of his argument depends on the accuracy of his hypothesis concerning the etiology of homosexuality and that that hypothesis has not been confirmed by empirical evaluations of experimental data. Such evaluations, of course, postdate Freud.

Psychohistorians today, however, have no excuse for proceeding to make analytic statements based on hypotheses that are at best unconfirmed and at worst disconfirmed.

For an example more recent than Freud, we might turn to the psychohistorical work on Hitler, surely the psychohistorian's favorite subject to date, although Richard Nixon may be fast catching up. The analyses of Hitler differ from one writer to the next, but a theme that commonly occurs in the work of most writers concerns the psychoanalytic defense mechanism of projection. Projection, to use Walter C. Langer's definition in the original psychoanalysis of Hitler, "is a technique by which the ego of an individual defends itself against unpleasant impulses, tendencies, or characteristics by denying their existence in himself while he attributes them to others." It is now commonly held that Hitler's anti-Semitism (with its roots in his early childhood) was in large measure the result of projection: "Because Hitler's hatred of the Jews was monumental," writes Robert G. L. Waite, "his feelings of guilt and self-loathing *must have been* very great indeed."[23] This is, of course, possible and perhaps plausible, as are any one of a number of hypotheses. But as a simple minimal requirement for accepting the notion of projection in any particular psychohistorical explanation, we should have some solid evidence indicating that the mechanism itself exists. We do not have such evidence. To be sure, common sense and everyday experience tell us that something *like* projection *seems* to exist; but "something like" it is quite different from the specific *psychoanalytic* meaning of the term, which derives from Freud's insistence that projection is inextricably linked to the development of paranoia.[24] Empirical efforts to confirm the existence of this postulated mechanism have failed to do so.[25]

As we will see in a later chapter, empirical testing of various psychoanalytic hypotheses has confirmed some, has disconfirmed others, and has sometimes found the hypotheses too vague or too premised on other disconfirmed ideas to permit adequate testing. It should not be asking too much of would-be psychohistorians to suggest that they at least familiarize themselves with these empirical studies before they employ what are all too often clearly mistaken—if marvelously imaginative—products of Sigmund Freud's creative genius.

Problems of culture. One of Freud's failings in his study of Leonardo, we have seen, involved a lack of familiarity with certain conventions in artistic expression prior to and during Leonardo's lifetime. There are other examples of this in his book that were not mentioned earlier. For example, in establishing the image of Leonardo's contradictory personality, Freud takes as evidence of Leonardo's gentleness his habit of buying and freeing caged birds. What Freud failed to note, however, was that this practice is a very old and popular folk custom that was believed to bring good luck.[26] This is not to deny that Leonardo was often gentle and kind but merely to point out that what appears to the modern reader to be evidence of one characteristic may in fact be entirely explicable in *other* terms if one simply knows enough about the cultural world inhabited by the subject. This is just common sense to the traditional historian; indeed, understanding cultural context is one of the basic and preliminary tasks involved in the writing of history. Cultural context is, however, something repeatedly ignored in the writing of most psychohistory. An example to illustrate this point can be found in a recent psychobiography of Thomas Jefferson.

In *Thomas Jefferson: An Intimate History* Fawn Brodie makes much of Jefferson's involvement with his young slave, Sally Hemings. The story of Jefferson's alleged intimacy with Hemings is not new; it has been a matter of gossip for a century and a half and was examined with care, thoroughness, and sensitivity by Winthrop Jordan only six years prior to the publication of Brodie's book. But Brodie is interested in something more. She is intrigued with the idea that Hemings was a "special preoccupation" of the Virginian, with the depth of his love for the "forbidden woman," and with the relationship of this preoccupation to his "inner needs." Thus, she finds in his journal of a trip through Holland, while Hemings was supposedly on his mind (though there is, of course, no evidence for this), descriptions of the landscape that include fully eight references to the color of the land as "mulatto." Brodie contrasts this journal with a similar journal Jefferson kept earlier, "just before Sally Hemings' disturbing mulatto presence had come to trouble him," and finds that the word mulatto appears but once. (Actually, the word appears twice.) This and other "psychological evidence" of Jefferson's supposed obsession, including such telling items as his designing a plow (with its "ancient symbolism") during the fateful trip and his reference in a letter to an ironic tale concerning noses (which is seen as *possibly* the only nonwhite trait possessed by Hemings), mean much to Brodie the analyst. Unfortunately, Brodie the historian had not done her homework.

As Garry Wills has pointed out, the word "mulatto" was commonly used by eighteenth-century Americans to describe the color of soil—as were red, gray, reddish-brown, and black, which Jefferson also used frequently in his journal. But why did "mulatto" appear four times as often in the *later* journal? Perhaps for the same reason that "red" appeared more than five times as often in the *earlier* journal: the trips covered substantially different terrain and the soils were *in fact* different in color.[27]

If this sort of silliness were confined to Brodie's book, it would be merely (to use one of her own favorite words) curious; but it is not. All of the books mentioned in the previous several pages share, in varying degrees, the problem of making much of matters that are notable only for their lack of singular importance once they are placed in their cultural context. All of them also share all of the other problems that have been pointed out. The studies of Luther, Jackson, Hitler, and Jefferson all build complex arguments on virtually nonexistent evidence; all violate elementary rules of logic in developing those arguments; and all analyze data using theories that fail to withstand empirical examination and experimental testing.

This should not be surprising, for all of these works are guided by a collection of hypotheses—one version or another of psychoanalytic theory—that itself suffers from problems of illogic, experimental nonconfirmation, and cultural parochialism. To examine this problem more closely is the task of the following chapters. In the first of these chapters, however, another element is introduced. What I have called "problems of fact" is not something that can be removed from the examination of specific historiographical applications of theory. Something of a parallel does exist, nonetheless, between the problem of fact in history writing and the problem of therapy in psychoanalyzing. History writing begins with the accumulation of data; the most basic test of a work of history is whether or not the facts "work" when shaped into an argument. Psychoanalytic theory begins with therapy; the most basic test for a theory grounded in clinical therapeutic experience is whether or not that theory "works" when applied to therapy. Thus, the first of the four chapters that make up the middle section of this book concerns itself with the fundamental question: does psychoanalytic therapy work?

2

"What—no wooden legs?"

—Anatole France,
on viewing the discarded
crutches and other medical
paraphernalia at Lourdes.

The Problem
of Therapy

SOME say that one of the common characteristics of the aged person of genius is a susceptibility to depression.[1] Whether or not this is a demonstrable fact need not concern us at the moment. Let us assume it to be true. Let us further assume that depression was a problem encountered late in life by someone of interest to the psychohistorian—say, Goethe. What can be made of this fact? How can we find out the cause of this condition? We might try common sense: according to Ortega y Gasset, Goethe was caught in a constant struggle with himself over how to live his life, and his alleged depression was one sign of his "living contrary to his vocation."[2] But this is perhaps too simple, too superficial an explanation—at least for those who seek "deeper" answers. Let us then turn for assistance to someone of expertise in curing such maladies as depression.

His name is Digat Anak Kutak. He studied for many years in preparation for his occupation as therapist among the Iban people of

Borneo, and he has an excellent reputation. If presented with the problem of Goethe's depression (or anyone else's, for that matter), he would have a ready diagnosis: Goethe's soul had obviously been stolen by an evil spirit. Should we betray some pessimism with regard to this judgment, Digat could readily assure us that years of successful clinical experience had led him to such a conclusion, a conclusion held by all the other therapists known to him. In short, repeated good fortune in the curing of depression—by covering himself with a blanket, journeying to the realm of the spirits, recapturing the lost soul, and blowing it back into the patient's skull—has convinced Digat and his colleagues that they know the cause and the cure of this problem. After all, he would perhaps reason, if they were wrong about the cause of the affliction their therapy could not work; since the therapy does work (and even Western authorities agree that it does), they must be right about the cause.[3]

I think it fair to say that, despite Digat's assurances, most historians would still be skeptical of an account that soberly blamed soul-stealing evil spirits for a historical figure's mental troubles. Even the most open-minded among them would ask for more evidence than that provided by the Iban therapist's private clinical experience. What sort of evidence would they want? Well, are there any statistics supportive of the therapist's claim—statistics on his actual cure rate, on his cure rate compared with that of other forms of therapy (e.g., primal screaming, devil exorcism, animal magnetism, psychoanalysis), or on his cure rate compared with that afforded by an *absence* of therapy? This would be a beginning.

To be sure, even if it were found that the Iban therapist's efforts were far more (or less) successful than any other form of therapy, the presence (or absence) of soul-stealing evil spirits would still not definitely be indicated. To establish or reject the entire system of causation and explanation would require evidence of a quite different sort. Since, for extraneous reasons such as therapist suggestion, Iban therapy might succeed *despite* the *non*existence of the posited spiritual world (just as the therapy may fail though the spiritual world may exist), testing of the efficacy of that therapy could not fully confirm or deny the proposition that Goethe was depressed because his soul was stolen. Should such tests show Iban therapy to be greatly superior to other forms of therapy, however, further investigation would at least be called for. If, on the other hand, Iban therapy were shown to be inferior to other forms of therapy, at the very least a deeper skepticism concerning the explanatory power of the Iban therapist's causal system (those soul-stealing evil spirits) would seem equally warranted.

But this is not a book about Iban therapy. It is about psychohistory—in practice, psychoanalysis as applied to history. Still, the same questions remain. Psychoanalysis is at base a therapeutic method. Its formal data derive from clinical experience, and its primary practical application is to clinical work. Further, as with Digat Anak Kutak, in his efforts to cure, the psychoanalyst claims to be encountering the forces of an invisible world—those demons residing in the unconscious. Should we ask a psychoanalyst to explain Goethe's alleged depression we would be equally obliged to ask him the same questions we asked the Iban therapist: since your explanation is at least initially based on your experience in therapy, how well does your therapy work? If it works well, fine, we can go on from there with our evaluation of the total system of psychoanalytic explanation; and if it fails to work well, then it must be considered thenceforth with at best a very skeptical attitude.

*   *   *

We must begin by acknowledging that psychoanalysts do not at all appreciate "outside" efforts at scrutinizing and evaluating their clinical activities. Indeed, they insistently claim that statistical studies cannot do justice to the subtlety of their ideas and the uniqueness of each case. Thus, following Freud, they most often argue that rather than using large-scale scientifically controlled experiments to determine the validity of psychoanalytic therapy "it is wiser to examine one's individual experiences."[4] This is the sort of behavior, when roles are reversed, that the analyst labels "resistance." And it is worthy of note that this attitude was rather late to develop in Freud. Earlier in his career, when Freud was much more optimistic about the positive effects of his therapy, he welcomed and even boasted of what he considered experimental confirmation of theory.[5] In any case, to reject experimental investigation out of hand is tantamount to admitting that psychoanalysis is not a science or even a coherent body of replicable procedures: to deny in advance the efficacy of experimentally testing the value of therapeutic techiques is, ipso facto, to strip them of scientific pretension.

Even if we ignore this problem, however, and attempt to do what the analyst wishes—that is, accept only the information he or she provides us—a battery of further difficulties is in store. The first of these is the fact that different psychoanalysts, confronted with identical typescripts of an analytic session, show great difficulty in agreeing on interpretations of that session.[6] This is caused by the fact that in the absence of objective and verified data analysts are free to emphasize one aspect of psychoanalytic theory and deemphasize or disregard others, as Freud well knew. Thus, at a time when Karen Horney's early criticisms of his ideas regarding female sexuality were gaining adherents, Freud observed: "We shall not be very greatly surprised if a woman analyst who has not been sufficiently convinced of the intensity of her own wish for a penis also fails to attach proper importance to that factor in her patients. But," he then casually added, "such sources of error, arising from the personal equation, have no great importance in the long run." With this dismissal Freud provided a classic example not only of the evidentiary hollowness typical of his theories, but of the remarkably prescientific and even primitive fashion in which debates among analysts are resolved: analyst "prestige and authority," coupled with "enthusiasm, persuasiveness, or even just plain dogmatism . . . without any check" determine the outcome of such disagreements. Or so says at least one analyst who should know, since he served for sixteen years as Director of Research for the London Institute of Psychoanalysis.[7]

Another matter of concern, at least to anyone who might wish to make general extrapolations from the psychoanalytic encounter (as the psychohistorian does and must), is the extraordinary degree of demographic bias that is present. Various studies have shown this to be true. The patients of psychoanalysts tend to be mostly white, predominantly Jewish, relatively young, exceptionally affluent, highly educated, and very well informed as to the nature of analytic therapy. One study even reported that fully *half* of the patients surveyed were themselves "engaged in work related to psychiatry and psychoanalysis."[8] To use this population sample to generalize about contemporaries who do not fit this demographic profile is certainly dubious; to use it to generalize about people who lived and died centuries ago borders on the absurd—but more about that in a later chapter.

Not only is the psychoanalytic patient strikingly nonrepresentative of the population at large in terms of race, religion, age, income, and education, he or she is also nonrepresentative of the total population *in therapy* of one sort or another. This is because of the highly selective criteria applied in the screening of prospective patients. Studies have shown, for example, that as few as *four percent* of patient applicants may be accepted for treatment and that those accepted are much less disturbed to begin with than those who are accepted by nonpsychoanalytic therapists. A report on the outcome of psychoanalytic treatment in the Columbia University Psychoanalytic Clinic, for example, concedes that the only people admitted to treatment were those who, after careful screening, possessed "sufficient motivation" for improvement and who showed, before treatment, a favorable prognosis based on a "symptomatology of a relatively short duration" and a capability of "effective functioning, either currently or in the recent past."[9] In other fields of therapeutic endeavor this would be called stacking the deck. In psychoanalysis it is, and always has been, common practice.

But there is more. Psychoanalysts make it very difficult to evaluate the outcome of therapy, even on their carefully selected patient population, by insisting on two totally unacceptable ground rules. The first of these is that the inquirer must accept the analyst's own judgment as to his degree of success or failure. Even on its face this provision would be unsatisfactory because of the possibility of distortion, both accidental and intentional, but it is made all the more unacceptable by the evidence that such distortion is not only possible but common. Analysts have been shown, for example, to be more likely than other therapists to perceive positive change where none existed in fictitiously constructed and taped therapy session "excerpts" alternately labeled "early" and "late," and they are more likely than other therapists to perceive interviewees as "significantly more disturbed" when presented as "patients" than when described as "job applicants."[10] Further, and this is true of therapists of various persuasions, there is evidence that they may be *twice* as likely as their own *patients* to declare a treatment a success, despite the fact that placebo studies invariably show that patients report improvement even when no "legitimate" therapy has taken place.[11]

The second unacceptable ground rule insisted upon by the analyst is the definition of a "complete" analysis. To the psychoanalyst a treatment is complete only when it is successful—no matter how long that takes. As Stanley Rachman has observed, it is thus possible that a patient who discontinues analysis after seven unsuccessful years (say, 1500 hours) "would be regarded as a premature terminator rather than as a failed case."[12] By using this sort of semantic sleight-of-hand the American Psychoanalytic Association has been able to report a success rate (as determined by their analysts) of over 95% among a surveyed sample of patients who completed analysis, while blandly noting that at least half the patients in the survey did *not* complete the therapy.

In point of fact, this APA study began with a sample population of ten thousand patients whose profiles had been provided by members of the Association. For some unexplained reason each follow-up inquiry resulted in a dramatic failure of the majority of originally participating analysts to submit reports, and eventually a total of 595 neurotic patients was determined. Of these, 289 (or 49%) "did not complete" the treatment. That left 306. On further inquiry only 210 of the 306 patients were reported on; of these, *35 patients* were reported to be fully cured (that is, symptom-free), while the remaining 175 ranged from "cured," but with residual symptoms remaining, to "improved." On the basis of *these* results the Association concluded that "about 97% of the patients who undertake analysis for neurotic reactions and 'complete' it, are 'cured' or 'improved.'"[13]

Surely, this will not do. Perhaps, since it was Freud who first directed that any inquiries regarding the efficacy of analysis focus on individual cases, we will do better by looking at his own therapeutic record. Freud's writings cover a span of more than half a century of work, filling the pages of nearly two dozen books and well over a hundred papers in addition to his voluminous correspondence. These writings include pronouncements on a staggering variety of themes ranging from slips of the tongue and the meaning of jokes to the history of humankind and the future of religion—all drawing from and elaborating on, in one way or another, his psychoanalytic method. It may then come as a surprise to some that in all this writing Freud discussed at length no more than half a dozen of his own cases, all of which were handled within a relatively short period of time: the cases known as Dora (1905); Little Hans (1909); Lorenz, or Rat Man (1909); Schreber (1911); Wolf Man (1914); and the female homosexual (1919).

On closer examination, however, as Michael Sherwood of the

Harvard Medical School has pointed out, even this small number must be qualified. Dora was treated only briefly with no discernible positive effect. Little Hans only met Freud once, very briefly—the entire "analysis" having been carried out by the boy's father, a close follower of Freud. Lorenz was a complete and apparently successful analysis. The Schreber case was only a historical reconstruction based on published memoirs. The Wolf Man case dragged on for many years, with different analysts and resulted in the eventual apparently paranoid breakdown of the patient. The female homosexual, like Dora, quickly terminated after virtually no attempt at treatment and with no effect. Thus, as Sherwood notes, "only the Lorenz case is a complete analysis," and even with it there are possible problems of therapist suggestion.[14]

Of course, Freud did *see* many more patients than this. A thorough search of all his works by one researcher has turned up 145 cases of at least passing mention in his writings.* But, for whatever reasons, Freud chose not to discuss most of these cases at length. It is little wonder that in the most recent and rather friendly large-scale survey of psychoanalytic theory and therapy, Seymour Fisher and Roger Greenberg are forced to admit, with delicate understatement, that "Freud chose to demonstrate the utility of psychoanalysis through descriptions of largely unsuccessful cases" and that he "never presented any data, in statistical or case form, that demonstrated that his treatment was of benefit to a significant number of patients he himself saw."[16] In short, if we accept Freud's advice that it is only the individual cases that matter in evaluating the merits of psychoanalytic therapy, we must conclude that his own self-selected and reported therapeutic record hardly inspires confidence.

---

* It should be noted that these cases showed precisely the same sorts of demographic bias that would become the rule for psychoanalysis. For example, the vast majority of Freud's patients were upper-class females and, in his entire reported case load, only two patients were beyond the age of forty-five; of those twelve patients who received more than cursory mention, *nine* were between the ages of eighteen and twenty.[15]

This modest conclusion is reinforced when we observe that there is evidence indicating that the use of hastily trained college students and even psychiatric *patients* as therapists can produce positive clinical results superior to those reported by Freud and equal to or better than that obtained by modern professional therapists of various persuasions.[17] In addition, other forms of therapy frequently report anecdotal success (admittedly, like that reported by psychoanalysts, unverified) at least as impressive as Freud's: scream therapy, dance therapy, pet therapy, "rage" therapy (which involves "physical stimulation of the rib cage area"), shopping therapy, "rebirthing" (extended snorkeling in a hot tub), computer therapy (talking to a computer programmed with a vocabulary of set psychiatric interview questions such as, "Is that the real reason?"), "direct" therapy (which is an all-out emotional assault often requiring that the therapist lie to, cheat, humiliate, terrorize, and possibly insist on sexual intercourse with the patient), jogging therapy, and, of course, the much more substantial therapies of shamans, priests, and witchdoctors. So far, however, no one has seriously attempted a work of psychohistory using the findings of these therapies as a theoretical underpinning.[18]

It seems clear that for a large number of theoretical and substantive reasons no resolute investigator can assent to the psychoanalyst's admonition that he or she examine only those cases the analyst cares to divulge and accept in those cases the analyst's own criteria for evaluation. As even some longtime friends of Freudian theory have begun to recognize, to maintain this traditional stance is to only further damage the already sullied reputation of psychoanalysis. Thus, for example, Hans H. Strupp, in an address to his colleagues in the Council of Psychoanalytic Psychotherapists, has complained of the "failure of psychoanalysis to have cultivated a spirit of open inquiry," of its treating "its theories, techniques, and insights as a secret lore, a kabbala, open only to the initiated" and has lamented the fact that "to put it bluntly, psychoanalysis has lost its scientific respectability."[19] Into this troubled state of affairs the examination of experimental and statistical data might seem like a breath of fresh air; it might even, as Fisher and Greenberg suggest, "do a great deal for the self-feeling of analysts."[20] It might. But whether it does or not, that is where our inquiry must now take us.

*　　*　　*

During the 1930s and 1940s a number of studies were carried out that either directly concerned or were relevant to the evaluation of psychoanalysis and other forms of psychotherapy. The results were printed in various professional journals where they lingered for years, causing barely a ripple of concern in the therapeutic community. But then in 1952, Hans J. Eysenck, the outspoken and iconoclastic University of London psychologist, published a five-page paper in the *Journal of Consulting Psychology* that caused that community to erupt in shock and outrage. Probably the single most frequently quoted title in the literature on therapy evaluation during the past quarter century, Eysenck's little paper initiated debates that continue today and that form the starting point for virtually every effort to assess the value of psychotherapy.[21]

What Eysenck did in his paper that was so upsetting was to draw on those earlier studies, involving a total of over seven thousand patients, to make an admittedly crude attempt to establish a rate of "spontaneous remission" from neuroses—that is, a rate of recovery without benefit of psychotherapy—and then to compare that rate with reported recovery rates of patients who had received psychotherapy. He found that the available studies all pointed in one direction: there appeared to be "an inverse correlation between recovery and psychotherapy" of any sort, and as for psychoanalysis it showed the worst recovery rate of all approaches, and by a very wide margin.

Psychotherapy, and particularly psychoanalysis, appeared in fact to be a *danger* to mental health, its main effect iatrogenic—a term used to describe illness *caused* by medical care. In this initial calculation Eysenck classified those patients who had stopped treatment without improvement as therapeutic failures. However, recognizing what he referred to as "the peculiarities of Freudian procedures," he recalculated his figures to give the benefit of the doubt to psychoanalysis by considering only "the percentage of completed treatments which are successful." This resulted in a psychoanalytic improvement rate of approximately 66%, about the same as with other forms of therapy and slightly less than that for patients who had received no formal treatment at all.

Eysenck's most generous conclusion, then, which caused such an understandable furor among psychotherapists, was that "roughly two-thirds of a group of neurotic patients will recover or improve to a marked extent within about two years of the onset of their illness, whether they are treated by means of psychotherapy or not." Further, "this figure appears to be remarkably stable from one investigation to another, regardless of type of patient treated, standard of recovery employed or method of therapy used."

One of the first responses to Eysenck indicates the sort of confusion his paper wrought. Noting that "it is obvious that some people change in some ways under the influence of some kinds of therapeutic activities while other people do not change, or change in different ways, under the same therapeutic activity, and that still other people change in ways similar to the above without any therapeutic activity," this incisive writer urged that the wisest reaction to Eysenck's challenge was to make believe it hadn't happened.[22] His colleagues understandably did not heed the advice.

Since the amount of writing on this topic now runs into many thousands of pages, we obviously cannot treat it here in any detail. Nevertheless, certain main lines of argument stand out. The first of these arguments concerns the concept of spontaneous remission. Analysts and their supporters claim that the studies Eysenck used to calculate the spontaneous remission rate were inappropriate for that purpose because of variations in the criteria used to determine improvement and because the supposed non-treatment control groups often did receive *some* sort of palliative care, though not formal therapy.

The question of improvement criteria is one that may never be satisfactorily answered so long as we accept the therapists own evaluations of their work. Apart from the problem of bias already discussed, there is the matter of agreeing on a definition of success. To take one admittedly extreme example, the form of treatment known as primal therapy claims it has attained success when the patient has a significantly lowered interest in work, politics, sex, and activity in general. Thus, one cited instance of therapeutic success is a Ph.D. candidate in English who now reads nothing but fairy tales. Of other patients surveyed in a follow-up study by Arthur Janov, the founder of primal therapy, "nearly all . . . said that they had much less sex than before" and in fact "do less, go less, want less, talk less— everything is less."[23] Not surprisingly, there have been some skeptics who have questioned whether such affectless, alienated placidity is to be considered a desirable sign of health.[24]

In contrast, the criteria used in the studies consulted by Eysenck to locate the phenomenon of spontaneous remission ranged from the hospital discharge rates of diagnosed neurotic patients who received only custodial care to the self-reported ability of individuals who had been receiving disability insurance for neurotic disorders, but had not undergone psychotherapy, to return to work, function socially, and remain symptom-free. Though far from ideal (as Eysenck admitted), these criteria were at least based on relatively objective data that were accessible to outside scrutiny. If anything, these criteria may have been biased against recovery, since the hospitalized patients were possibly more disordered than the others, and the patients on disability insurance were to some extent being encouraged to remain unwell. But whatever the bias problems in Eysenck's calculations, subsequent studies using much tighter controls (such as actuarial analyses of clinical work and comparisons of patients treated therapeutically with those who, though diagnosed as in need of treatment, were left to linger on therapists' waiting lists) have supported the claim that spontaneous remission is a genuine phenomenon—though actual rates of remission and therapeutic success have fluctuated.[25]

The other criticism, that Eysenck's (and others') nontreatment control groups did receive *some* care—though not psychotherapy—is usually linked to the conclusion, arrived at by Leo Subotnik, that "there is no evidence that improvement is *a function of time,* as the hypothesis requires."[26] This criticism simply misses the point, as it confuses "spontaneous" with "uncaused." Certainly the control groups received *some* treatment. Eysenck admitted as much when he noted that the patients in at least one of the studies he consulted "were regularly seen and treated by their own physicians with sedatives, tonics, suggestion and reassurance . . . the stock-in-trade of the general practitioner." They may also have benefited from spousal comfort, financial windfall, or any of a number of personally helpful experiences—or, they may not have. Eysenck's point was not that, left to their own devices, under even the worst environmental conditions, neurotics would necessarily improve as "a function of time"; it was, simply, that *in the absence of formal psychotherapy* a certain percentage of persons afflicted with neuroses would still show improvement and that the rate of improvement would be at least comparable to that attained by formal psychotherapy. The first part of this argument, that at least *some* persons would recover without psychotherapy, now appears beyond dispute—as even common sense would dictate. To argue the contrary is to take the position that in all of human history before the invention of modern psychotherapy neurosis, once developed, *never* disappeared. The second part of the argument remains in a state of debate; that is, how does the rate of spontaneous remission compare with the success rate for psychotherapy? We don't yet have a precise answer. But we do know that, at best, the difference is not great, if it exists at all.

Thus far we have only discussed the arguments that have taken place regarding spontaneous remission and psychotherapy in general. What about *psychoanalysis* as therapy? How does *it* compare, in terms of success rate, with no treatment and with other forms of therapy? Here, there is less disagreement and we can draw conclusions more easily. Even among those researchers who insist that therapy of one sort or another for neurotic disorders is more beneficial than no treatment at all (including simple custodial care) and who accept the psychoanalyst's insistence that unhelped treatment dropouts don't count, there is general agreement, according to Fisher and Greenberg, that "psychoanalysis has not been shown to be significantly more effective than other forms of psychotherapy with any type of patient" and that therefore "there is at present no justification for a patient to assume that he will achieve a greater degree of improvement in a therapy called psychoanalysis than in a therapy given another label such as analytically-oriented, client-centered, or behavioral."[27]

As for the contention that through the process of transference the psychoanalytic patient gains "insight" that leads to more lasting change than that attained by other forms of therapy (something that even Freud expressed doubts about near the end of his career), the most sanguine view—again that of Fisher and Greenberg—is that this "has not yet been demonstrated" and that it is in fact contrary to "a voluminous empirical literature" indicating that "the application of direct behavioral techniques without any attempts to promote insight" produce changes that "do not usually appear to result in either substitute symptoms or shorter-lived cures."[28]

This, as I say, is the generous view. Others—behaviorists, generally—point to a significant body of experimental literature in concluding that, in Rachman's words, "there is still no acceptable evidence to support the view that psychoanalytic treatment is effective."[29] In a 1973 review of the twenty-year accumulation of research that followed his original paper, Eysenck is more definite: "the evidence is completely congruent with a view that if psychoanalysis has any effects over and above spontaneous remission, these cannot be large or important, if they exist at all." He adds that, although this conclusion is always subject to reconsideration in the face of new evidence, the indications at present are all negative, and he notes that "certainly there is no hypothesis in experimental psychology which would still be maintained by any serious worker if so much negative evidence were available to contradict it."[30]

Subsequent work in the field continues to provide this "new evidence"—and also to support Eysenck's general contention. For example, an extensive, sophisticated, and well-controlled recent study conducted at the Temple University Psychiatric Outpatient Clinic rated a group of patients who had received behavior therapy, a group who had received analytically oriented therapy, and a group of wait-listed controls who received no formal therapy at all. Initial patient assessments were made and compared with later follow-up assessments to establish degrees of specific and overall improvement. While the two groups of treated patients appeared to improve at a similar rate (the behavior therapy subjects showed slightly greater overall success), and both of them at a somewhat greater rate than the non-treatment group, by the conclusion of the study over fifty percent of the wait-list group were considered "improved or recovered symptomatically." But even this validation of a high rate of spontaneous remission was biased in favor of the treatment groups—first, because all subjects "wished to receive psychotherapy" and the wait-list patients received frequent assurances "that

they were not forgotten and would soon be assigned to treatment";
second, because the final assessments were arrived at by combining
the evaluations of the patients themselves, their therapists, and psy-
chiatrically trained outside assessors who were kept uninformed as
to the treatment (or non-treatment) categories of individual patients.
In the opinion of just this latter group—surely the most objective
measure—*all three* groups improved dramatically and with no significant differences among them.[31]

Studies of this sort continue to be done, generally producing support for Eysenck's overall argument, but also invariably generating
disagreements concerning a wide variety of specific sub-problems.
Faced with these sorts of disagreement, what is the layman to conclude? The most prudent response, obviously, is to avoid taking
sides on the specific issues that remain a matter of serious professional debate. That is what we shall do here. But at the very least we
can find it instructive that so limited a number of major issues are in
fact still genuinely problematic. The arguments now center on
whether or not psychoanalytic therapy has a greater rate of success
than that accomplished by no formal therapy at all. There is wide-
spread agreement that psychoanalytic therapy is, at best, no more
successful than any other therapeutic technique. Even Freud seems
finally to have come to recognize this fact. Only a few years before
his death, and perhaps in anticipation of the final pessimistic
thoughts on psychotherapy that he would express in "Analysis Terminable and Interminable," he wryly observed: "I do not think our
cures can compete with those of Lourdes. There are so many more
people who believe in the miracles of the Blessed Virgin than in the
existence of the unconscious."[32]

Freud need not have looked to so exotic an example as Lourdes to
draw such a gloomy conclusion. The somewhat comparable recovery rates of psychoanalysis, non-psychoanalytic psychotherapy, and
spontaneous remission are also about the same (actually, a bit lower)
as those achieved for *all* patients—not only a careful selection of

what we would call neurotics today—at the Friend's Asylum in Pennsylvania during the middle years of the nineteenth century.[33] In those unenlightened days the guiding therapeutic technique at the most successful institutions was "moral treatment"—kindness, trust, encouragement, and respect directed toward the promotion of self-esteem. As Stanley Rachman suggests, "it may turn out, in the long run, that psychotherapy does no more than provide the patient with a degree of comfort while the disorder runs its natural course."[34]

* * *

It is not the purpose of this chapter to dissuade those in need from seeking professional advice, nor to suggest that such people would do just as well to talk with a witch doctor or a college student or a psychiatric patient about their problems, although in individual cases, it seems, that *may* be good advice. (There is little doubt that in many cultures witch doctors are more successful than any Western psychotherapist might be—and one cannot but find troubling the report in a famous study by D. L. Rosenhan that a group of feigned mental patients in a variety of public and private institutions were readily identified as such by other "legitimate" patients while the resident psychiatrists persisted in treating the feigned patients as schizophrenics.)[35] We are not concerned here with therapy except as it concerns evidence for the validity or nonvalidity of a total system of behavior explanation that may be useful in helping us understand the lives of historical figures. But in those terms all the evidence does support one conclusion: there is no reason to believe, based on its therapeutic usefulness, that psychoanalytic theory is better than any other theory for the conduct of historical inquiry. On this evidence, at least, there appears to be no reason for the discriminating reader to even seriously entertain the explanatory notions of the psychohistorian, or at least to give them more credence than any other explanations.

As indicated at the beginning of this chapter, disconfirmation of therapeutic efficacy (whether of psychoanalysis or witch doctoring) does not *necessarily* imply disconfirmation of the total system of explanation in question, any more than confirmation of therapeutic efficacy would necessarily confirm the validity of that system. But, though not sufficiently determinative to confirm or deny by itself the theoretical foundations on which psychohistorical analyses are built, the lack of evidentiary support for psychoanalytic therapy is hardly irrelevant.

In an essay on the scientific stature of psychoanalysis written twenty years ago, the philosopher Sidney Hook remarked that he was "sorely puzzled that some psychoanalysts seem inclined to dismiss the question of therapeutic efficacy as an irrelevant intrusion into the evaluation of its truth claims. It is as if," he went on, "a meteorologist dismissed the significance of his daily weather predictions as irrelevant to his science."[36] No doubt there are times when meteorologists wish they *could* do just that—and for the same reason that psychoanalysts *do* do just that. The credibility of meteorological theory, however, would obviously be seriously diminished if such an attitude were generally maintained. In the case of psychoanalysis the situation is more extreme. To continue the comparison, it is as if meterologists not only dismissed the relevance of their daily weather predictions, but also insisted on the scientific nature of their endeavor while *denying* others *access* to their predictions. I think it is clear that major questions would be raised if, in addition to such efforts at concealment, it were subsequently found out (as it has been with regard to psychoanalysis) that the predictions of meteorologists were in fact no more accurate than those of any other weather predictors—say, the local drug-store almanac or even the proverbial man in the street.

I will strain the analogy no further. Psychoanalytic theory has other problems deserving of our attention.

3

"I don't know what you mean by 'glory,'" Alice said.
Humpty-Dumpty smiled contemptuously. "Of course
you don't—till I tell you. I mean 'there's a nice knock-
down argument for you!'"
"But 'glory' doesn't mean 'a nice knock-down argument,'" Alice objected.
"When *I* use the word," Humpty-Dumpty said in a rather
scornful tone, "it means just what I choose it to mean—
neither more nor less."
"The question is," said Alice, "whether you can make
words mean so many different things."
"The question is," said Humpty-Dumpty, "which is to
be the master—that's all."

—Lewis Carroll,
*Alice's Adventures
in Wonderland*

The Problem
of Logic

DURING the course of a 1963 symposium on philosophy
and history, the historian Bernard Bailyn considered some of the
matters under discussion—"the problems of objectivity and subjec-
tivity, the involvement or detachment of the inquiring mind, the
nature of facts, and the predictive value of historical knowledge"—
and wondered aloud "whether, if what one is concerned with is the
actual problems of the working historian, he should be talking
about such matters as these at all."[1] Had they known of this remark
multitudes of "working historians" no doubt would have ap-
plauded Bailyn's words.

But if philosophy has generally found a cool reception among
historians, its reception among members of the psychoanalytic community has more often been truly glacial. In a general sense this is so
because of the field day philosophers of science have had with the
scientific pretensions of psychoanalysis. In a more specific sense it is
so because in their multi-faceted attacks on the pretentiousness of

psychoanalysis many philosophers have gone so far as to argue that the very core subject of psychoanalytic concern—the unconscious—does not even exist. It is here, then, that any consideration of the logical status of psychoanalytic theory must begin.

Freud has, time and again, been hailed as the "discoverer of the unconscious." This is inaccurate, of course, as Freud himself recognized. "The poets and philosophers before me discovered the unconscious," he once acknowledged (indeed, he might have added, the word itself—at least as Freud used it—was coined by Coleridge); "what I discovered was the scientific method by which the unconscious can be studied."[2] This discovery, no mean achievement in itself if correct, was accomplished, first, by turning what had traditionally been a nonsubstantial quality or concept into an actually existing "thing." For Freud and his followers the unconscious thus became "something actual and tangible," "a mental province," an "abode" of imaginary essences, a "special realm" of activity—to use phrases Freud himself used on numerous occasions. To his famous and probably most devoted disciple, Ernest Jones, Freud's great accomplishment was locating and examining the nature of "a strange mental world quite foreign to that of consciousness. . . . [a] buried stratum of the mind . . . extremely primitive in nature, and closely akin to the mind of both the infant and of the savage."[3]

The unconscious became, in short, an actual place into which things (ideas, fears, desires) were deposited and hidden. This place, to the psychoanalyst, filled as it is with all manner of forgotten experiences, is of especial importance to the individual. It is, in fact, the primary force behind all mental activity and as such is singularly fundamental to psychoanalytic theory. By literalizing what he himself admitted was but a "façon de parler" to his predecessors, Freud in a sense repeated the process that Franz Anton Mesmer had pioneered a century earlier: he *invented* a substance (Mesmer called his substance *fluidum*) and then claimed to be able to understand and

control its functioning.[4] But most philosophers remain unconvinced of its existence.

Gilbert Ryle has referred to the psychoanalytic idea of the unconscious, and to all such ideas rooted in the Cartesian conception of a
body-mind dichotomy, as "the dogma of the Ghost in the Machine."
Such dogma, Ryle says, is a "logical howler" that derives its existence from a massive "category mistake."[5] He illustrates this point
with reference to a series of hypothetical situations. One of them
asks the reader to imagine a foreigner watching his first game of
cricket:

> [He] learns what are the functions of the bowlers, the
> batsmen, the fielders, the umpires and the scorers. He then
> says, "But there is no one left on the field to contribute
> the famous element of team-spirit. I see who does the
> bowling, the batting and the wicket-keeping; but I do not
> see whose role it is to exercise *esprit de corps.*" Once
> more, it would have to be explained that he was looking
> for the wrong type of thing. Team-spirit is not another
> cricketing-operation supplementary to all other special
> tasks. It is, roughly, the keenness with which each of the
> special tasks is performed, and performing a task keenly
> is not performing two tasks. Certainly exhibiting team-
> spirit is not the same thing as bowling or catching, but
> nor is it a third thing such that we can say that the bowler
> first bowls *and* then exhibits team-spirit or that a fielder
> is at a given moment *either* catching *or* displaying *esprit
> de corps.*[6]

In the same way, Ryle and others have argued, for an individual to
"have" a particular character trait means that one has a *tendency* for
a certain type of *behavior*; brusqueness, amiability, suspiciousness,
and the like are not substantive entities that one can actually possess.
Thus, as Alan R. White writes:

Because acquiring knowledge, or traits, or habits, is not thus analogous to acquiring material possessions, the ability to produce our knowledge, or the tendency to manifest our traits and our habits, does not imply the existence of a place where the as yet unproduced knowledge, or unmanifested traits and habits, is kept—in the way that the ability to produce a notebook does imply the existence of a place in which the notebook is kept when it is not in use. There is no more an answer to the question "Where is my knowledge when I am not recalling it?" than there is to the question "Where is my conceit when I am not displaying it?" Whether or not I am always, or ever, conscious of my habit of dropping my aspirates, it is a mistake to suppose that, when that habit is not at work, it has either disappeared or is being kept hidden in some place, perhaps a psychical place.[7]

The problem of mind-body dualism has had a profound influence on the philosophic problem of "other minds," a corollary of the philosophy of mind debates that have concerned a great many analytic philosophers since Wittgenstein. The "other minds" problem grows directly out of the skepticism implicit in Descartes' questioning of his own existence and, indeed, has roots dating back at least to Plato's question in *Theatetus*: "Are you quite certain that the several colors appear to a dog or to any animal whatever as they appear to you? . . . or that anything appears the same to you as to another man?" As two recent philosophers have put the problem: "What justification, if any, can be given for the claim that one can tell, on the basis of someone's behavior, that he is in a certain mental state?"[8]

The answer of the skeptic is that no justification at all can be given, since mental and physical states are different things. To determine another's mental state on the basis of his behavior is, they say, impossible. The only reliable way of determining another's mental state is through direct, shared experience of that state; as that is logically impossible, the skeptic claims, it follows that it is impossible to reliably determine the mental state of another person.

Since humans spend much of their lives and predicate much of their behavior in determining the mental states of others, however, this skepticism has understandably troubled philosophers. The traditional rejoinder some philosophers have given the skeptic has been based on an argument from analogy. Though constantly rephrased and refined, essentially the argument rejects the impossibility of determining another's mental state on the basis of his or her behavior and claims that either by repeated observation of one's own physical reactions to particular mental states or by observation of the reliability of others' repeated determinations of one's own mental states on the basis of their reactions to one's own observed behavior, a fairly reliable model can be constructed to enable determination of another's mental state on the basis of his or her behavior. But the endlessly problematic nature of such a determination—to say nothing of the assumption in both the argument of the skeptic and in that of the answer by appeal to analogy of the viability of the mind-body dichotomy—has resulted in the rejection by most philosophers of both the skeptical argument and the argument from analogy. In their place one form or another of philosophical behaviorism has generally been substituted.

As subject to revision and modification as is the argument from analogy, the behaviorist argument has an equally fundamental disagreement with the skeptical position. Those who accept the argument from analogy deny the impossibility of determining another's mental state on the basis of his or her behavior; those who accept the behaviorist argument deny the essential *difference* between mental and physical states. The purely mental phenomena of the mind-body dualist, most behaviorists point out, are by definition private and inaccessible to study; therefore, it is argued, they are at best unintelligible, at worst nonexistent. Unconscious mental states are seen as a contradiction in terms: what is "mental," the critic points out, is by definition conscious. Speculations on the existence of something called the unconscious are—*and can only be*—nothing more than speculations, speculations rendered unnecessary by behaviorist theory.

In brief, the more radical behaviorists deal with the "other minds" problem simply by denying its problematic nature as usually stated. Thus, Rudolf Carnap writes, "a sentence about other minds states that the body of the person in question is in a physical state of a certain sort." Since, in Carnap's words, "a sentence says no more than what is testable about it," any assertion about another person's so-called "inner state" of being is nothing more than "a metaphysical pseudo-sentence."[9] Not all behaviorists would agree with such an extreme position, and not all critics of body-mind dualism are behaviorists. All such opponents of the Cartesian dichotomy, however, behaviorists or not—and they represent the vast majority of philosophers—either implicitly or explicitly deny the existence of the "Ghost in the Machine." They approach the problem of "other minds" by directing themselves solely to evidences of behavior and/or language. J. J. C. Smart speaks for a substantial, if perhaps radical philosophic community, when he suggests "that even the behavior of man himself will one day be explicable in mechanistic terms. There does seem to be, so far as science is concerned, nothing in the world but increasingly complex arrangements of physical constituents."[10]

What has all this to do with psychohistory? Simply this: if the logical critique of the philosophical behaviorist is accurate, psychoanalytic theory, founded as it is on the requisite existence and nature of the Freudian unconscious, must collapse. And with the collapse of psychoanalytic theory goes the essential underpinning of psychohistorical explanation.

As the psychological behaviorist would be quick to point out, however, the collapse of psychoanalytic theory would not require the abandonment of explanation for phenomena allegedly explained by the psychoanalyst, since for every psychoanalytic explanation there is a behavioral counter-explanation. This is important in logical terms since it has become something of a scientific axiom that theories are never thoroughly undermined merely by criticism, but only by the development of superior theories. A case in point that the behaviorist might use is Freud's famous *Analysis of a Phobia in a Five-Year-Old Boy*—the case of "Little Hans."[11]

The case of Little Hans has long been recognized as one of Freud's most important case histories. It is repeatedly cited in the psychoanalytic literature as a seminal proof of the validity of psychoanalytic theory. Edward Glover, for one, calls it "one of the most valued records in psychoanalytical archives. Our concepts of phobia formation, of the positive Oedipus complex, of ambivalence, castration anxiety and repression, to mention but a few, were greatly reinforced and amplified as the result of this analysis."[12]

Hans was a five-year-old boy referred to Freud because of the "nonsense," or phobia he exhibited concerning large animals—especially horses. The immediate precipitating experience was the child's witnessing the fall of a horse drawing a bus in the street, although the boy had undergone at least two prior negative experiences involving horses. As noted in the last chapter, Freud actually carried out his analysis with the boy's father as intermediary, a man who was enthusiastically familiar with Freudian theory and who went to great lengths to elicit involuntary admissions from Hans and to interpret the "actual meaning" of vague and ambiguous language. (For example, he reports a response of "Hm, well," to a leading question concerning the boy's affection for his sister as flatly "assenting.")

It is impossible to outline the entire process of Hans's analysis here or to go into it in any detail, but in the end Freud concluded that the fundamental source of the boy's phobia was repressed Oedipal anxiety. "Hans was really a little Oedipus," Freud writes, "who wanted to have his father 'out of the way,' to get rid of him, so that he might be alone with his handsome mother and sleep with her."[13] He had "transposed from his father on to the horses" his jealousy and hostility. The phobia thus gave the five-year-old boy an excuse to spend more time with his desired mother:

> The content of his phobia was such as to impose a very great measure of restriction upon his freedom of movement, and that was its purpose. . . . After all, Hans's phobia of horses was an obstacle to his going into the street, and could serve as a means of allowing him to stay at home with his beloved mother. In this way, therefore, his affection for his mother triumphantly achieved its aim.[14]

Hans's phobia eventually disappeared with the resolution of his Oedipal conflicts, Freud concluded: Hans imaginatively married his father to his father's mother, "instead of killing him. With this phantasy both the illness and the analysis came to an appropriate end."[15]

There are, to begin with, some serious—if basic—*evidentiary* problems with this analysis. Psychohistory enthusiasts, such as Hans Meyerhoff and H. Stuart Hughes, frequently claim that history and psychoanalysis have a strikingly similar goal: "to liberate man from the burden of the past by helping him to understand that past."[16] This may be so, but one can only wonder what a properly skeptical historian would think of such "evidence" as the constant interpretation of a five-year-old subject's *real* meanings by a father who saw himself as the object of the boy's antipathy (of which nothing was directly reported by the boy himself) and a man whom Freud regarded as "among my closest adherents." On several occasions when Hans (what the historian would call the "primary source") made a statement unsupportive of the psychoanalytic theory being used to analyze his case, his father would parenthetically insert for the official record such characterizations as "hypocritical" or "disingenuous." And finally, there is the following admission by Freud:

It is true that during the analysis Hans had to be told many things which he could not say himself, that he had to be presented with thoughts which he had so far shown no signs of possessing and that his attention had to be turned in the direction from which his father was expecting something to come.[17]

Freud's justification for this sort of procedure, which, as others have pointed out, runs throughout his work,[18] would be cold comfort to the historian:

This detracts from the evidential value of the analysis but the procedure is the same in every case. For a psychoanalysis is not an impartial scientific investigation but a therapeutic measure. Its essence is not to prove anything, but merely to alter something.[19]

Had Freud been consistent in this latter view, psychoanalysis and psychohistory would doubtless be very different fields today; but on more occasions than not, particularly as the early claims of therapeutic efficacy began to appear increasingly dubious, Freud actively claimed therapy-transcendent scientific status for his work.

The purpose of examining this case, however, is less to dissect it or compare its regard for rules of evidence with that common among historians than it is to contrast its explanatory system with that of the behaviorist. In 1960 a non-psychoanalytic interpretation of the case of Little Hans was published.

Joseph Wolpe and Stanley Rachman devote much of the space in their reconsideration of the case to a review and criticism of Freud's analysis. This criticism is of less importance to the present study than is their own counter-explanation of the boy's phobia. All phobias, they claim, "are regarded as conditioned anxiety (fear) reactions. . . . If the fear at the original conditioning situation is of high intensity or if the conditioning is many times repeated the con-

ditioned fear will show the persistence that is characteristic of neurotic fear."[20] Citing evidence that a single experience can induce a
phobia, the authors take Hans's words at full value when he says to
his father: "No. I only got it [the phobia] then. When the horse in
the bus fell down, it gave me such a fright, really! That was when I
got the nonsense." Although the data provided are insufficient for
full non-psychoanalytic analysis, Wolpe and Rachman note that
the gradualness of Hans's recovery is consistent with the frequent
spontaneous decline and disappearance of phobias in children
reported by many researchers. Gradual refamiliarization with the
phobic stimuli in nonthreatening situations has been shown time
and again to be highly successful phobia therapy. The authors suggest that the repeated discussions of the incident were helpful in
acquainting Hans with his particular phobic stimuli, thus perhaps
easing the anxiety factor, but they claim that the excursions into the
hypothetical world of the Oedipus complex were of no direct therapeutic value.

The obvious fundamental difference between the psychoanalytic
and the behavioral explanations of Hans's phobia, for the general
purposes under discussion here, is that between Freud's belief in the
dynamic importance of repression and the unconscious and Wolpe
and Rachman's considerably more mechanistic view of phobia ac-
quisition and recovery. Given the accuracy of the premises underlying each explanation and discounting specific evidentiary problems,
the details of each theory seem reasonably consistent and complete.
The key, then, to determining the most satisfactory explanation
must reside within those basic premises. Some of the difficulties in
accepting the psychoanalytic model have already been reviewed; the
behavioral model is not without difficulties of its own.

Behaviorists, as we have seen, have been critical of the psychoanalytic conception of the unconscious as a studiable entity because it is
by definition private and directly inaccessible; its very existence can
only be hypothesized. But the psychoanalyst may readily reply that

this is not by any means sufficient grounds for denying the existence of the unconscious. Perfectly legitimate scientific work is carried out every day by physicists who can do no more than posit the existence of critically important submicroscopic entities. The empirical validity of their scientific work rests on the efficacy of the entire theory surrounding these unobservable quantities. Various "imagined" entities, such as the unobservable particles assumed, and even physically described, as part of the kinetic theory of gases—or the so-called "gluons" of recent quantum chromodynamic theory—are the everyday objects of scientific study. What matters is not whether such entities are or are not themselves detectable, but whether the theory of which they are an essential part can be empirically substantiated. William P. Alston makes this point succinctly in a passage that deserves quoting at length:

> There is a commonly accepted doctrine, largely derived from a consideration of physics, according to which a theory involving unobservables gets empirical significance by virtue of the fact that it, together with subsidiary assumptions, implies various general law-like hypotheses which can be directly tested empirically. In this way the theory can be assessed in terms of the extent to which it succeeds in explaining and unifying a variety of lower-level laws which have been empirically confirmed, and on the negative side, the extent to which it does not imply lower-level hypotheses which have been empirically disconfirmed. The Bohr theory of atomic structure, which represents an atom as a sort of miniature solar system with electrons revolving in orbits around the nucleus, cannot be tested directly, for an individual atom cannot be observed. However, from the theory we can derive a variety of testable hypotheses—for instance, those concerning the constitution of the spectrum of the light emitted from a given element.[21]

Of course, the example of the atom—and most other such unob-servable entities in science—is quite different from the unconscious in that the atom is *in principle* observable though submicroscopic, whereas the unconscious logically is not. Nevertheless, to temporar-ily ignore this important point, what then remains pragmatically crucial is not the behaviorists' objection to the mysteriousness of the concept of the unconscious, but whether the theory growing out of this postulated entity is empirically verifiable. This is the subject of the next chapter. The behaviorist model has other problems, how-ever, that deserve recognition before we turn to the question of the empirical validity of psychoanalytic explanation.

The philosophic problem of "other minds," discussed earlier, deals a sharp blow to the Cartesian dualism of body and mind and in the process seriously undermines the foundations of psychoanalysis. The primary counter-explanation, which is behaviorism, is not gen-erally accepted as free from serious flaws of its own, however. Per-haps the most direct problem of behaviorism is its defiance of the common sense belief, rooted in virtually all cultures, of the body-mind (sometimes called body-soul) dichotomy.[22] Behaviorism has failed to shake the intuitive conviction of most people in the exist-ence of a self beyond the mechanistic self of behaviorist theory. Pop-ular belief may or may not be sufficient reason for doubting its validity, and in purely logical terms it clearly is not, but behavior-ism is undeniably saddled with a common reaction against its ideas that recalls Bertrand Russell's words on the skeptic's approach to the "other minds" problem:

> We are not content to think that we know only the space-time structure of our friends' minds, or their capacity for initiating causal chains that end in sensations of our own. A philosopher might pretend to think that he knew only this, but let him get across with his wife and you will see that he does not regard her as a mere spatio-

temporal edifice of which he knows the logical properties but not a glimmer of the intrinsic character. We are therefore justified in inferring that his skepticism is professional rather than sincere.[23]

As to the specific problem of "other minds," radical behaviorism has never successfully freed its theory from the elementary criticism that humans are possessed of the ability to deceive other humans. The principle that the body-mind dichotomy is fallacious implies the ability of one individual to determine another individual's mental state merely by close observation of his or her behavior. This ability would seemingly deny the possibility of successful pretense, a denial of such questionable validity that the problem of "other minds" is very far from resolution. While modifications of behaviorism have in many ways blunted the full force of this basic objection, in one form or another it continues to haunt the philosophical behaviorist.[24]

Certain logical underpinnings of behaviorism are, it thus seems, almost as flawed as the logical premises of psychoanalysis. Behaviorism cannot, then, be generally regarded as the superior theory which could completely supplant the questionable explanatory approach of psychoanalysis, except insofar as behaviorism does not require the elaborate untestable hypotheses of psychoanalysis. This simplicity is not, however, insignificant. Since at least the fourteenth century, the importance of the principle of parsimony in explanation—known, after its most prolific user, as "Ockham's razor"—has been widely recognized in philosophy. The principle that "what can be done with fewer assumptions is done in vain with more" and its modern version as a thoroughly accepted philosophic dictum that "entities are not to be multiplied without necessity" is a powerful argument for the logical superiority of behavioral theory—one that has not been lost on proponents of psychological behaviorism.[25] The problems that psychoanalytic theory purports to explain can be explained at least equally well by behaviorism; and since behaviorist explanation is dependent on far fewer questionable assumptions, the behaviorist can quite properly assert that it is the superior of the two theories.

The critic of psychoanalysis who hopes to reach a general audience, however, must recognize the realities of the everyday world, and in that world the principle of parsimony is simply insufficient to thoroughly undermine psychoanalytic theory. The notion of the unconscious, however logically problematic, does easily appear to satisfy, in a popular common sense way, questions raised by phenomena ranging from dreams to forgetfulness to slips of the tongue. Thus, whether or not there actually is such a thing (or place) as the unconscious, logical argument appears at present to be capable only of raising serious questions about it. There are not yet adequate grounds for outright rejection of the concept, no matter how philosophically dubious it may appear. This does not, of course, mean that behaviorism is "wrong"—or that all or any of the further ramifications of psychoanalytic theory are "right"—but merely that until the opponents of body-mind dualism have made their case considerably more convincingly, the existence and nature of the Freudian unconscious must remain an open question, at least in the everyday world of the nonlogician.

*   *   *

The attention thus far paid to the logical status of the Freudian unconscious is not meant to suggest that it is the only aspect of psychoanalytic theory that is logically problematical. The logical status of the concept of the unconscious is the most central and complex issue, but other logical problems abound. They include the problem of refutation and the *post hoc, ergo propter hoc* fallacy.

It is a widely recognized postulate of philosophic and scientific practice that unless a theory can *in principle* be refuted it must be rejected as having no claim to scientific legitimacy. In other words, any theory that can explain everything—that is irrefutable because it is incapable of being negated by contradictory observational evidence—effectively explains nothing. As Ernest Nagel has succinctly put it, for a theory of any sort to be logically credible "it must *not* be formulated in such a manner that it can always be construed and manipulated so as to explain whatever the actual facts are, no matter whether controlled observation shows one state of affairs to obtain or its opposite."[26] An example that is commonly used to illustrate this point, since its initial elaboration by Karl R. Popper, is the contrast between astrology and Einstein's gravitational theory. One of the key reasons why astrology fails to measure up to the scientific standards of Einstein's theory is *not* that it is not capable of confirmation. Quite the contrary. As Popper noted, astrologers, "by making their interpretations and prophecies sufficiently vague . . . were able to explain away anything that might have been a refutation of the theory had the theory and the prophecies been more precise." Unlike Einstein's theory, which is subject to refutation, astrological theory, has about it an intentional semantic vagueness that is like a room made of mirrors which endlessly confirms its own reflections. In Popper's words: "In order to escape falsification [astrologers] destroyed the testability of their theory."[27] Since it is thus not in principle subject to refutation, astrology is neither scientific nor even logically respectable. That psychoanalytic theory is subject to criticism on these same grounds can best be seen by example.

One of the psychoanalytic concepts most heavily used to date both by psychohistorians and by those anthropologists who have attempted psychoanalytically to interpret complex cultures from a distance, is the hypothesis of anal-erotic character traits. The anal-erotic hypothesis is of central importance in Bruce Mazlish's psychobiography of Richard Nixon, in Walter C. Langer's and Robert G. L. Waite's studies of Hitler, and in the wartime work of Geoffrey Gorer

and Weston La Barre on Japanese character, to name but some of the
most prominent examples.[28] In her recent psychoanalytically informed biography of Thomas Jefferson, Fawn M. Brodie opens the
first chapter with a recitation of Jefferson's character traits that
might have been borrowed from a psychoanalytic textbook. Jefferson,
it seems, was unusually "acquisitive," "controlled," and "orderly" to
such a degree "that it can be properly called compulsive." Geza
Roheim, in typically grand style, has gone so far as to characterize
all of Western culture as anal. And in an early study Owen Berkley-
Hill, though not quite so ambitious as Roheim, expressed a similar
opinion regarding much of *Eastern* culture: repressed anal erotism,
he argued, was the principle source of Hindu character and behavior.[29] Such an extraordinarily pervasive condition might at first
seem to suggest that those who have applied the concept to specific
cases have distorted it to fit their purposes. If so, the problem would
reside not with the concept itself, but with such individual applications of it. This, however, is not the case.

Arising from conflicts surrounding childhood toilet training, the
anal-erotic character is traditionally associated with such traits as
frugality, obstinacy, and orderliness, and anal traits supposedly have
a certain sadistic element associated with them as well.[30] All such
character traits, however, are marked by the latent possibility of a
"reaction-formation" which can produce behavior precisely the
opposite of that noted above. Thus Ernest Jones, in his classic explication of the anal-erotic character, explains that one feature of the
anal personality "is the extraordinary and quite exquisite tenderness
that some members of the type are capable of, especially with children . . . [as a result of] the reaction-formation against the
repressed sadism that so commonly goes with marked anal erotism."
Further, as well as manifesting "the impulse to gather, collect, and
hoard" ("all collectors," Jones writes, "are anal-erotics"), the anal
personality may be marked by the opposite impulse:

Such people, so far from being proud of their possessions
and productions, take very little interest in them. They
are often quite indifferent to their immediate surround-
ings, to their furniture, clothes and so on. As to their own
productions, whether material or mental, their chief concern after the process is finished is to get rid of them as
completely as possible, and they discard them with no
wish to know what becomes of them.[31]

In brief, an individual (or a culture) may be described as anal-
erotic if he or she (or it) exhibits traits of frugality or generosity,
orderliness or disorderliness, sadism or kindliness. Since all such
traits are marked by a continuum from one extreme to another, since
there is no quantitative device for measuring degrees of character
traits (although psychohistorians are often given to claims such as
that of Bruce Mazlish, who says he has "never dealt with a public figure *as ambivalent* as Nixon"),[32] and since all individuals commonly
display any or all of these characteristics to *some* degree at any given
time, it is possible to describe virtually anyone as anal-erotic without
distorting the theoretical concept of the anal-erotic character. So far
from being an effective mechanism for analyzing and explaining
human character, then, the anal-erotic hypothesis is logically and
analytically useless. The concept is in principle irrefutable. Because
in theory it is all inclusive, can accommodate any set of facts sup-
plied, and potentially explains everything, in truth it is powerless to
effectively explain anything.

The logical failing of the anal-erotic character is not an isolated
weakness of psychoanalytic theory. In addition to reaction-formation, the defense mechanisms of sublimation, repression, and denial
(all essential to psychoanalytic procedure) permit the psychoanalyst
to posit the existence of traits and attitudes for which there is *no positive evidence at all*, thus making a specific analysis logically irrefutable. Yet, one cannot examine a work of psychohistory, regardless

of the talent or stature of the author, without encountering the effects of this crippling logical failing. It appears in such narrow and detailed work as Kurt Eissler's attempt to rescue Freud's analysis of Leonardo (he argues that because of the presence of defense mechanisms, Freud is correct whether or *not* the infamous bird was a vulture, whether or *not* the Caterina in Leonardo's journal was his mother, and so on) and extends to such grandiose efforts as Jay Gonen's attempt to psychoanalyze Zionism (reaction-formation accounts for the alleged fact that "the self-image of Israelis can shift from schnorring beggars into people of dignity").[33] Further, in camouflaged form the same logical principle appears in Erikson's *Childhood and Society* in which he argues that a person's or a nation's "identity" is derived from a counterpointing of opposite potentialities. And this insight in turn led to, among other works, Michael Kammen's borrowing of the Eriksonian principle to produce an irrefutable and therefore sophistical analysis of American culture by examining the "biformities" allegedly peculiar to America's "contrapuntal civilization."[34] In the hands of those writers—unlike Erikson and Kammen—whose imaginations seem to know no restraint at all and who (to cite but one case) find psychoanalytic meaning in the fact that Richard Nixon one day ate corned beef hash with an egg on it, the logical elasticity of psychoanalytic theory attempts to make a virtue of what G. K. Chesterton long ago recognized as the "sin and snare" of biographers: the tendency "to see significance in everything; characteristic carelessness if their hero drops his pipe, and characteristic carefulness if he picks it up again."[35]

"It is a typical soothsayer's trick," Karl R. Popper writes, "to predict things so vaguely that the predictions can hardly fail; that they become irrefutable." Any theory that rests on such perfectly circular logic is, as Popper has repeatedly shown, more "myth" than scientific hypothesis.[36] And any theory that is more myth than scientific hypothesis—that becomes retrospective soothsaying in the hands of the historian—is a very questionable base for historical explanation. For jokes of a certain sort, however, such logical circularity is ideal. An example is the one retold by analyst Edgar A. Levenson that is, he says, "well known in psychiatric circles":

> It is said that this family constellation—that is, an aggressive, domineering, seductive mother and a weak, passive, undermining father—is characteristic for the alcoholic. But this is also the classic Jewish family structure. So, it is asked, why are there so few Jewish alcoholics? The answer is—of course—their mothers won't let them![37]

For reasons of avoiding logical circularity of another sort, I will avoid noting here what Freud had to say about this type of joke.

*   *   *

The logical objection of *post hoc, ergo propter hoc* is one to which historians should be acutely sensitive, since, in their everyday work with severely limited data, this fallacy is virtually an occupational hazard. Although mentioned briefly in an earlier chapter, it is worth discussing a bit more fully here. David Hackett Fischer has shown, for instance, how the defeat of the Spanish Armada in 1588 has been seen by numerous historians as the "cause" of events ranging from the decline of the Spanish empire to the flowering of Elizabethan drama—and how in each case the only actual evidentiary support for such proposed causality lies in the *post hoc, ergo propter hoc* fallacy.[38] But if the traditional historian must be wary of such errors in logic, the psychohistorian raises the odds almost to the point of certainty that he will fall prey to the fallacy, since he is adding to the pitfalls of historical analysis an explanatory system that has itself rarely addressed and has never dealt adequately with this dilemma to which it is intimately tied.

Murray G. Murphey, one of the more sophisticated and penetrating thinkers to have addressed problems concerning the relationship between history and the social sciences, attempted in 1965 to use psychoanalytic theory to generalize about the group character of a certain body of early-nineteenth-century residents of the mid-Atlantic United States. Murphey consulted a large body of autobiographies, child training manuals, and travelers' reports in an attempt to arrive at an accurate description of child-rearing practices during the period under study. He hoped to correlate the child-rearing data with adult attitudes expressed in the autobiographies and then to sketch the prevailing personality type of his subjects. The autobiographies were not helpful in ascertaining the nature of child-rearing practices, and the child training manuals and travelers' reports, Murphey recognized, were too class-biased to permit useful generalizations. In an attempt to deal with this absence of reliable information on child rearing Murphey compiled a profile of expressed adult attitudes from the autobiographies and then—taking at face value psychoanalytic theory concerning the relationship between child training and adult personality—used these attitudes as a means to "discover" the otherwise elusive child-rearing practices. If the adults expressed certain specified attitudes, Murphey assumed that they *must have* undergone certain specified childhood experiences. Then finally, since his subjects (according to psychoanalytic theory) must have undergone these early experiences, the experiences themselves (though wholly imaginary) became causal explanations for the perceived adult attitudes.[39]

Although in principle Murphey's study is logically flawed, and seriously so, it might be argued that it is not necessarily *wrong*. Every individual makes frequent decisions and evaluations based on incompletely proved presumptions of causality, and quite often such decisions and evaluations prove correct. If a historian uncovers demographic information suggesting that at a certain place and at a certain time food supplies dropped drastically and then subsequently finds evidence of looting in the marketplace of that area soon after the food shortage broke out, he or she might well theorize—barring any contradictory evidence—that the looting resulted from the food shortage. Despite the fact that strictly speaking this would be *post hoc, ergo propter hoc* reasoning, most other historians would probably not find serious fault with the hypothesis—barring, of course, specifically contradictory evidence. This would be because numerous other examples exist in which people have responded in a similar manner to conditions of sudden and drastic deprivation. The looting hypothesis would thus seem analagous to other empirically verified situations.

If Murphey had been able to point to a body of empirically verified studies showing that individuals possessing the attitudes found in his autobiographies had in fact undergone the childhood experiences which he hypothesized, his conjecture would be on firmer ground. That he could not refer to any such studies is not his fault. For the most common approach in psychoanalytic work is to do precisely what Murphey did—to read back from evident adult characteristics to assumed or "reconstructed" childhood experiences. Each case thus treated becomes the evidentiary base for subsequent analyses, although none of the cases in question has any firm empirical foundation. Popper makes this point neatly in describing an encounter he once had with Alfred Adler:

> Once, in 1919, I reported to him a case which to me did not seem particularly Adlerian, but which he found no difficulty in analysing in terms of his theory of inferiority feelings, although he had not even seen the child. Slightly shocked, I asked him how he could be so sure. "Because of my thousandfold experience," he replied; whereupon I could not help saying:"And with this new case, I suppose your experience has become thousand-and-one-fold."

What I had in mind was that his previous observations
may not have been much sounder than this new one; that
each in its turn had been interpreted in the light of "previous experience," and at the same time counted as additional confirmation. What, I asked myself, did it confirm? No more than that a case could be interpreted in the
light of the theory. But this meant very little, I reflected,
since every conceivable case could be interpreted in the
light of Adler's theory, or equally of Freud's.[40]

Obviously, this procedure is logically treacherous. Just how treacherous it can be, however, can best be seen in one final example.

In a wartime study of the Japanese character structure Geoffrey
Gorer attempted to account for what he referred to as "the most
paradoxical culture of which we have any record." Although brightly
tinged with an understandable wartime xenophobia, the paradoxes
he observed and hoped to explain are worth quoting at length:

How can the same culture—often the same persons—
prize and perform the elaborate, highly ritualized and
symbolic Tea Ceremony, with its elegance, calmness and
poetry, and indulge in the almost unbelievable savagery,
lust and destruction of the rape of Nanking? Go out by
the hundreds of thousands to admire the wild cherries in
bloom or to listen to the cicadas, and at the same time sys-
tematically and consciously force whole populations into
the degradation of drug addiction? Hold serious lyrical
poetry competitions, in which the Emperor is a contest-
ant, and build a shrine for the Living Bombs—three
soldiers who fastened themselves to a high explosive
bomb? Develop some of the most refined graphic arts we
know, and yet have a major portion of the work of their
most famed artists so pornographic that much of it has
never been seen in Europe or America? Adopt the most
elaborate complications of our modern society and yet

retain a view of the world—part political, part religious, part social—more consonant with an isolated and primitive tribe than with a major industrial nation?[41]

The first problem Gorer encountered in his analysis was strikingly parallel to that encountered daily by historians—the absence of available living subjects to examine and question. With the war in progress he had no opportunity to study the Japanese firsthand. Instead, he read as widely as possible in the relevant literature and supplemented his research "by interviews with some two score informants who were either wholly or partially Japanese, or who have had prolonged and intimate knowledge of Japanese life."[42] Still, generalized information on child-rearing practices was unavailable, so, in much the same fashion as Murphey twenty years later, and the psychohistorian in general, Gorer allowed anecdotal reminiscences and perceived adult behavior to serve as confirmation for his otherwise highly questionable hypotheses on childhood experience. A major focus of his study was on the correlation between the alleged Japanese practice of severe and early toilet training and such attributed adult character traits as an "excessive fear and dislike of dirt," the "emotional unimportance of food," an "emphasis on neatness and tidiness," a "constant urge to control the environment as completely as possible," and a "deeply hidden, unconscious and extremely strong desire to be aggressive." These, of course, are classic symptoms of the anal-erotic personality, so Gorer's hypothesis seemed to confirm itself: largely because of unfortunate childhood toilet training experiences, the Japanese people exhibited the paradoxical and seemingly bizarre behavior the anthropologist had set out to explain.

But the war ended. And here the parallel between Gorer's study and the work of the psychohistorian came to a close; the subjects he had been compelled to examine from afar became available for direct observation. Gorer's study had been published in the 1949 edition of D. G. Haring's *Personal Character and Cultural Milieu*. In

1956 a new edition was published containing two firsthand studies of Japanese child-training practices which showed convincingly that conventional Japanese toilet training was not particularly rigid, and Haring himself added a belated observation that in eight years of living in Japan he had failed to see any evidence of early or severe toilet training.[43] Gorer's article was quietly dropped from the new edition, a casualty of an all too rare empirical disconfirmation of a logically contorted psychoanalytic explanation. Not only had Japanese toilet training practices been shown to be quite respectably flexible, but three years earlier a massive study had been published that added insult to the injury: Whiting and Child's *Child Training and Personality: A Cross-Cultural Survey* had shown that the *American* middle-class group sampled in the study was particularly rigid in its toilet training practices and began such training a year and a half sooner than the median for all societies surveyed, "earlier than is reported for any of the primitive societies reviewed with the single exception of the Tanala."[44]

*　　*　　*

The logical status of psychoanalytic theory, and its offspring psychohistory, is clearly problematic at best. It is beset by serious challenges to its most fundamental assumption, the existence of the Freudian conception of the unconscious. It is unavoidably involved in continual violations of a cardinal rule for all scientific explanation, the need for theoretical refutability. And it has made a practice of falling into logical fallacies that confuse mere temporal relationships with causality.

Beyond these problems, though directly associated with them, is the crucial matter of accounting for individual differences among people who have similar or identical backgrounds. If this cannot be done successfully then the very best efforts of the very best psychohistorians become nothing more than empty clichés on the order of those concerning the temperaments of redheads, the joviality of fat people, or the various stereotypes commonly applied to this or that racial, religious, or national group. In short, if the psychohistorian cannot explain the occurrence of individual differences among people with similar backgrounds, he or she can explain little of value. In a review of Walter C. Langer's psychoanalytic explanation for Hitler's behavior, Robert Coles states the problem incisively:

> How did a wretched, deeply troubled, at times pathetic youth—the "neurotic psychopath" of this book—end up Führer of the Third Reich, a man not only possessed of authority and power but believed and heeded by millions? If not Hitler, might it have been someone else? If only Hitler, then surely it was not his "perversion" or his disordered mind (the province of the psychoanalyst) that accounts for his successes. . . . The Weimar Republic was full of such people; America has had its share: people who "identify" with various "aggressors"—and, having done so, get nowhere. As for psychological recovery or "transformation," psychiatrists can spend long, intimate months, if not years, with patients and not know why at a particular moment a person is suddenly, it seems, "better." In *retrospect*, we come up with formulations, explanations: such and such was "interpreted." We are less likely to mention the many times we have offered similar "insights" to other patients, even to the same patient, all to no avail.[45]

This same point has been made in reverse by Jacques Barzun. In his study of Leonardo da Vinci, Barzun reminds us, Freud had argued that his subject's habit of leaving work uncompleted derived quite directly from his (historically disputed) childhood abandonment by his father, which was a central cause of his (alleged) homosexuality. But how then, wonders Barzun, are we to explain Goethe, "who also found finishing difficult, though he grew up with two parents and was a fairly active heterosexual"?[46]

Another example comes from Erikson's work on Luther, in which the explanation for Luther's attitude toward death is traced to particularities regarding his father. But, Roland Bainton has asked, how, then, are we to explain Erasmus with his similar attitude but very different paternal background?[47]

Still another more complex and revealing variation on this problem can be seen in David Donald's famous argument that the people who became leaders of the American Abolitionist movement of the 1830s were drawn to reformist activity because in so doing they were in *fact* making an "unconscious attack upon the new industrial system" that was socially alien to them and that had made of them "an elite without function, a displaced class in American society." How did Donald arrive at this conclusion? He laboriously compiled various personal characteristics of the 106 people he determined to have been the "hard core" of antislavery leadership and found them to be mostly non-immigrants with a median age of twenty-nine, who came largely from rural, respectable, middle-class New England families of Congregational-Presbyterian background, and who had liberal arts educations and little connection with industrial activity. Thus, Donald concluded, in their contemporary social milieu these were socially "displaced" people—it then following that "basically, abolitionism should be considered the anguished protest of an aggrieved class against a world they never made."[48]

Apart from the many other valid criticisms that have been leveled at this study, one of shocking simplicity stands out: how do we explain the elementary fact that in New England in the 1830s there were a much larger number of non-immigrant, rural, middle-class, respectable, Congregational-Presbyterians who also had liberal arts educations and little connection with industry, but who, at around the age of twenty-nine did *not* become Abolitionists? For that matter, what about the non-Abolitionist *siblings* of the "hard core" group, with their *precisely* matched family backgrounds? Unless we can come up with a credible explanation for the fact that these people with matched personal characteristics did *not* become abolitionists, the background information Donald compiled on the abolitionists tells us nothing whatsoever about individual or group motivation. Indeed, all it does tell us is that Donald unwittingly fell prey to a fallacy almost invariably found in the work of astrologers, numerologists, and psychohistorians, the fallacy known to statisticians as "the enumeration of favorable circumstances."

Instances of this sort can be repeated without end, but the fact is, no one has been able to adequately deal with the truly crippling problems for psychoanalytic theory and psychohistory that are raised by these questions. One major statistical effort to do so, however, is worth some attention.

During the 1960s psychoanalyst Raymond Sobel carried out a detailed four-year study of 400 randomly selected families in rural New Hampshire and Vermont in an effort to determine, as he put it, "what went right" in the lives of women who were by all measures mentally healthy, but whose early lives were "indistinguishable from those of patients who broke down with schizophrenic illness, neurotic maladjustment, or just depression and despair."[49] A team of researchers collected data using personal interviews and a 600-item life history questionnaire. Each family was visited twice with an interval between interviews of twelve to eighteen months, and in most cases different interviewers carried out the follow-up inquiry. Over a million bits of life-history information were thus accumulated and analyzed. From this mass of information indices of childhood stress and adult mental health were drawn up. The twenty-five women with the greatest positive discrepancy between childhood and adult indices were then selected out, since "these cases were the ones who had suffered the most in childhood and who were the healthiest in adult life." A series of detailed quantitative and qualitative evaluations were then performed, using the remaining families as a control population, to determine any particular characteristics that might suggest causative differences in the group that had most successfully made the passage from childhood adversity to adult mental health. After all this analysis was complete, Sobel concluded that "no differences could be found": "there seems to be no significant correlation between the historical data and the eventual mental-health functioning of the individual, even though there is ample evidence of both early trauma and adult health."

Sobel found this statistical failure "frustrating." So, following the questionable psychoanalytic counsel that individual cases reveal more than statistical surveys, he turned to a close examination of a single case. The case he chose was that of a thirty-two-year-old housewife who had suffered an extraordinarily troubled childhood with severe economic and educational deprivation, parental physical and mental instability (including the hospitalization of her father for schizophrenia), constant parental quarreling, and the death of her father when she was ten, followed by placement in foster homes and the homes of relatives. The woman finally married, at age seventeen, a man with a similar background. This woman came from the study group of twenty-five who had on every score clearly surmounted what Sobel called their "traumatized" childhoods; but, he noted, "it would be easy to find an equal number from the controls with similar childhood pathology but who, instead, had maladaptation as adults." None of the statistical scales could explain the woman's adaptation nor could the personal interview material provide "any clue" as to the reasons for her success. Sobel finally wondered if his methodology was at fault (though it was immeasurably more sophisticated and careful than anything that has even been proposed by clinicians or psychohistorians), and in the end he was left with a platitude. He concluded the report on the study with no scientific findings, but instead with a famous quote from Tolstoi: "All happy families resemble one another; every un-happy family is unhappy in its own fashion."

This is not much help to the would-be psychohistorian. Sobel, after all, is a trained psychoanalyst and professor of psychiatry at Dartmouth University Medical School. Compared with the totally uncontrolled characterological and demographic biases of the sub-jects of psychohistorical inquiry—to say nothing of the tiny scraps of fragmented, impressionistic, anecdotal evidence (often of dubious authenticity) that the psychohistorian has to deal with—Sobel's sub-ject pool and personal data were incomparably balanced and com-prehensive. The fact that he was reduced to concluding his study by citing the wisdom of a nineteenth-century Russian novelist to ac-count for his failure to find *any* generalizations applicable to the people his research team had studied and analyzed makes the simple and straightforward questions of Coles, Barzun, Bainton, and others impossible to ignore. Stated simply, if each case is individual and the explanations that apply to one do not necessarily (if ever) apply to others, how can claims be made that psychoanalytic theory is even a very low-level "system" of explanation? And if, as the evidence now more than suggests, it is not a workable system—if there are too many variables to allow it to be so described because every case is unique—how can it ever be used profitably by historians, who *must* make generalizations while dealing with only scattered remnants of evidence? The answer is clear: it cannot.

Nevertheless, psychoanalytic critics of conventional "common sense" historical explanations frequently argue that traditional his-torical explanations are themselves *ad hoc* and unsystematic and that individual historians often create their own admittedly infor-mal theoretical models. How much better it would be, they con-tend, for historians to agree on and employ a single, informed theory of human behavior—preferably Langer's "coldly penetrating calcu-lus" of psychoanalysis.

In the abstract this argument appears to have merit. But first such a theory must be shown to exist and be logically and empirically credible. Otherwise we are merely adding to the confusion by substituting an unverified and quite possibly harebrained body of scientifically pretentious and logically reductionist explanation that stands a very good chance of being dead wrong for the sensibly diverse, modest, cautious, common sense, experientially derived wisdom of the traditional historian. That is hardly an improvement.

"Ancient books also recorded that students could study at night by the light of fireflies placed in a bag—but I had my retainers in Jehol collect hundreds of fireflies and place them in a big bag, and they didn't give out enough light to read a single character."

—K'ang-hsi,
Emperor of China

The Problem
of Theory

FREUD'S theory of the repressed Oedipus complex—in his words, a sufficient achievement to give psychoanalysis "a claim to be counted among the precious new acquisitions of mankind"[1]— borrowed its imagery from Sophocles' *Oedipus Rex*. What Freud failed to acknowledge was that more than the imagery was borrowed; the very process of discovery by individual patients also closely follows Sophocles' tragedy. In his famous "Analysis of a Phobia in a Five-Year-Old Boy," Freud referred to Little Hans as "a little Oedipus" after, under much parental prodding, the child grudgingly seems to have accepted his father's observation that he wanted his father out of the way in order to be alone with his mother. In the Greek play Oedipus too gained his inspiration from a respected outside source: it was on a special trip to Delphi that Oedipus was told by the oracle that he was fated to kill his father, marry his mother, and have children by her.

Apart from the important fact that in Sophocles' tragedy Oedipus eventually slew his father and married his mother while still genuinely unaware of their true identities, it is worth emphasizing that the entire sequence of events began with the oracle's *prediction* to the troubled young man. The same pattern holds with Freud's analysis of Little Hans (and with psychoanalysis in general), thus raising a serious question. By whatever variant—be it Karl R. Popper's idea of the *Oedipus effect,* referring to "the influence of a theory or expectation or prediction upon the event which it predicts or describes" or Robert K. Merton's *self-fulfilling prophecy,* "a false definition of the situation evoking a new behavior which makes the originally false conception come true"—one must consistently wonder about the influence of analyst suggestion on any and all psychoanalytic explanations derived from case histories.[2] And the fact that one must *continue* to wonder, after three-quarters of a century of psychoanalytic history, indicates a major difficulty in attempting to empirically verify the claims of psychoanalytic theory.

It is the very nature of the psychoanalyst's practice—the concentration on carefully chosen individuals with acknowledged emotional difficulties; the refusal (whatever the therapeutic reasons) to directly record the patient's conversations; and the reliance upon the analyst's own fallible memory in later recalling important aspects of the patient's testimony—that makes rigorous examination of psychoanalytic case histories virtually impossible. The enormous biases that are built into the psychoanalyst's distillations of his or her cases prevent non-psychoanalytic investigators from doing more than pointing out internal problems of logic and offering (as in Wolpe and Rachman's review of the case of Little Hans) any but the broadest of counter-explanations. As with the question of therapeutic efficacy discussed earlier, if the merits of psychoanalytic theory are to be validly assessed, it is clear that something other than individual case histories must be examined.

A second problem in submitting psychoanalytic theory to close investigation rests on the quasi-mystical nature of major parts of that theory. The concepts of the collective unconscious, the genetic inheritance of ideational tendencies (or "memory traces"), the life and death instincts, and the "pleasure principle" are among the aspects of psychoanalytic theory that reside beyond the range of observation or investigation, and are ideas not, in fact, much used anymore, even by analysts. The concepts of the Freudian unconscious and the tripartite division of the mind into id, ego, and superego are crucial to psychoanalytic theory and are fundamental to psychoanalytic practice, though these ideas too are equally beyond the range of empirical examination. For the purposes of this study, then, the former concepts can readily and properly be ignored. The latter concepts involving the existence and structure of the unconscious, must be left as problematic—not because there is any evidence to support them but only because eliminating them for lack of evidence would in itself suffice to make further inquiry unnecessary.

Of the remaining major parts of psychoanalytic theory, only those that have been and conceivably will be frequently used by psychohistorians will be reviewed in this chapter. Thus, for example, because of the general absence of extensive and reliable data on the dreams of historical subjects, including sufficient information on context, psychoanalytic dream theory will not be considered. What we will consider—by examining major experimental studies rather than individual case histories with their biases and uncontrollable variables—are the concepts of the Oedipus complex, the defense mechanism of repression, the psychosexual personality syndromes, the question of infant experience and personality determination, and the proposition that paranoid delusions are caused by projections of homosexual feelings. These concepts have been chosen because they are relatively susceptible to empirical testing, because they are potentially relevant to historical explanation, and because previous reviewers have claimed that these concepts represent the strongest confirmations of psychoanalytic theory.[3]

*   *   *

The Oedipus complex, which Freud claimed "may justly be regarded as the nucleus of the neuroses,"[4] essentially involves an
observed intense sexual attraction in young children for the parent
of the opposite sex and of jealousy and hostility directed toward the
parent of the same sex. The intensity of these feelings is thought to
be unmatched at any other point in life. The theory postulates a
peak of intensity during the "phallic phase" of development (between about two and a half and six years of age), followed by a resolution of the feelings with the beginning of the stage of latency. Freud
writes:

> While he is still a small child, a son will already begin to
> develop a special affection for his mother, whom he
> regards as belonging to him; he begins to feel his father as
> a rival who disputes his sole possession . . . The Oedi-
> pus complex can, moreover, be developed to a greater or
> less strength, it can even be reversed; but it is a regular
> and very important factor in a child's mental life, and
> there is more danger of our under-estimating rather than
> over-estimating its influence and that of the develop-
> ments which proceed from it.[5]

The reasons for the importance of the Oedipus complex, particularly for the psychohistorian, involve the claim that it is ubiquitous
and has a bearing on adult interpersonal relationships. For example,
since the complex may become "reversed"—that is, the tie may be
made between son and father, rather than son and mother—an adult
male's aggressive behavior toward other males may suggest that he is
defending against latent homosexual tendencies rooted in his Oedipal phase. Because the persecutory delusions of paranoid schizophrenia are claimed to be the result of repressed homosexuality (a

contention examined later in this chapter), it is clear that the ramifications of the Oedipal phase are of major consequence, if the theory can be shown to be valid.

An immediate problem encountered in attempting to test any aspect of the theory of the Oedipus complex is the possibility of inversion. As was true of the "reaction-formation" hypothesis discussed in the last chapter, the possibility of inversion tends to make the theory untestable, for whenever there is apparent failure of confirmation in individual cases the psychoanalyst is free to claim that what has been observed is Oedipal inversion. If, in other words, a male has great fondness for his mother and displays animosity toward his father (however covertly, for repression is another inevitable factor in the equation) psychoanalysis can claim that these emotions are based in his Oedipus complex. If, on the other hand, he exhibits dislike for his mother and a relative fondness for his father, psychoanalysis can equally claim that his attitude is rooted in his Oedipus complex, though in this case it is inverted. The existence of the Oedipus complex is thus spuriously "proven" by virtually any emotional feeling of any male for his mother or his father. However, in the specific case of the Oedipus complex this dilemma can be dealt with easily. The fact is that no psychoanalyst denies that by far the most common Oedipal reaction is one which involves heterosexual drives. If studies of sufficient magnitude and sophistication can be constructed, it must be hypothesized that the overwhelming majority of cases will show a heterosexual Oedipal tendency.

Viewed quantitatively, those studies which have explicitly addressed the question of the presence or absence of the Oedipal syndrome suggest that the tendency does not exist and that it is, in Robert R. Sears's words, "a sharply etched grotesquerie" against Freud's more perceptive descriptions and analyses of human development.[6] But an egalitarian attitude is not necessarily a virtue in evaluating empirical research. The *quality* of the studies Sears relied on in making this judgment is more important than the number of studies that supported his negative conclusion. And in one important respect the majority of those studies were qualitatively flawed. Most of the investigations considered in the Sears report simply asked subjects which of their two parents they preferred (though some did this more subtly than others) and in general arrived at conclusions suggesting that no significant distinctions appeared.[7] The psychoanalyst's obvious criticism was that such tests did not probe the unconscious, where the repressed feelings of affection and antipathy are said to reside. Recent tests have attempted to uncover more than consciously expressed feelings, and some of them have provided low-level support for the Oedipal hypothesis.

At least one study often cited in support of psychoanalytic theory, however, must be treated with a good deal of caution. A work published by Calvin Hall of the Institute of Dream Research, claiming to be "an empirical confirmation of the Oedipus complex," relies upon such uncontrollable and unverifiable data, such questionable fundamental assumptions (e.g., that male strangers in dreams *always* represent fathers), such sociological innocence (failure to consider the fact that most of the dream material analyzed was directly reflective of such everyday waking realities as the tendency for men to be more openly aggressive than women), and is so admittedly "committed" to "classical Freudian theory" that it cannot be regarded as fulfilling the criteria for acceptable empirical research.[8]

By far the best study supportive of the Oedipus complex to date is one carried out by Stanley M. Friedman, a student of Hall's, nearly thirty years ago.[9] Friedman devised a series of six methods by which a sample of 305 boys and girls, randomly selected from a suburban Midwest school district and evenly distributed by age from five to sixteen, would indicate their feelings toward each of their parents. One of the six methods employed a fairly direct question, similar to the techniques used by the studies cited in the Sears summary; the other five used considerably more sophisticated and covert techniques, all of them substantively unrelated. They included showing the children drawings of boys and fathers and boys and mothers, girls and fathers and girls and mothers, in situations in which generational conflict was a possible but not a necessary interpretation. In this example—as in all *except* the direct question—conflict themes appeared to be significantly higher between parents and children of the same sex. The method of direct questioning produced differences that could not be ascribed to more than chance. Thus, within the limits of time and place—the suburban Midwest in the late 1940s—Friedman's conclusions seem supportable. Although the great age diversity of the subjects dilutes the focus of the study from the Oedipal phase somewhat by introducing other possible factors concerning the problems of adolescence, there does appear to be at least a general correlation in child-parent attitudes similar to that predicted by the Freudian hypothesis, and "the fact that all techniques yielded significant results with the sole exception of the one which projectively asked for the preferred parent, would indicate that the reason for failure is the inadequacy of this method for uncovering Oedipal manifestations."[10]

A few years prior to the Friedman study an investigation based on a smaller sample (but one better focused and controlled as to age group) also used both direct and projective techniques, but concluded that Freud's hypothesis was contradicted.[11] Another more recent study which also used both direct and projective techniques, similarly failed to confirm the hypothesis.[12] While there is still disagreement on this matter, the overall conclusions of all experiments that have concerned themselves with young children, in the words of the recent and relatively uncritical Fisher and Greenberg survey, "have not delineated the kinds of shifts in attitude toward same-versus opposite-sex parents that Freud suggested would occur in the vicinity of the Oedipal period."[13]

Still, if only for the sake of argument, it is instructive to proceed *as though* the only study worthy of note was the one most supportive of psychoanalytic theory—that of Friedman. What does it tell us? We must recall that the theory of the Oedipus complex is multifaceted: it postulates that the complex derives from the child's jealousy of the parental performance of the sex act and, further, that there are specific adult personality patterns that arise from the repressed Oedipus complex. Neither of these matters was confirmed or even tested by Friedman, nor have they been successfully tested by anyone else. Friedman's findings can be seen, then, as possibly important, but very limited. They show that *in a particular cultural setting* support was found for the hypothesis that, though not openly admitted, boys of all ages show a greater degree of hostility for their fathers than for their mothers and girls from the same age distribution show a greater degree of hostility for their mothers than for their fathers. This is interesting, noteworthy, and potentially valuable information (though we must not forget that we have ignored here the majority of studies that contradict these findings), but it is a long way from confirming or even providing the claimed "strong support" for the full psychoanalytic concept of the Oedipus complex.

The question of the ubiquity of the Oedipus complex is one that has now been pursued, on and off, for half a century. In the 1920s Bronislaw Malinowski and Ernest Jones engaged in a well-known debate on the subject, Malinowski having been convinced by his anthropological fieldwork in the Trobriand Islands that the Oedipus complex was not universal. The psychoanalytic hypothesis was based on an assumption of "triangularity" in family relationships involving father, mother, and (for purposes of discussing the classic Oedipus complex) son. The situation in the Trobriands, Malinowski noted, was also triangular, but the triangle involved brother, sister, and sister's son. The Trobrianders did not recognize biological paternity, and the father of a boy was not seen as his guardian. Moreover, and it was on the basis of this observation that Malinowski founded his criticism of the Oedipal concept, the most common relationship between fathers and sons was one of closeness and affection, while ambivalence and hostility often characterized a boy's attitude toward his mother's brother.

Jones's replies to Malinowski covered a variety of matters, but the answer that has had the longest life is that in the Trobriands the hostility for the mother's brother is the result of a *displacement* of the antipathy that occurs in patriarchal and patrilineal societies. If this argument is accepted—and it widely is, despite the slippery logic involved—some support is regained for the minor thesis of universal generational conflict between boys and adult males. Irrevocable damage, however, is done to the central argument that the source of the Oedipus complex is sexual jealousy, since Trobriand husbands, wives, and children share a common abode from which the mother's brother is generally excluded, and there exist exceptionally strict incest taboos involving sisters and brothers. There is no sexual relationship between mothers and their brothers to account for the hostility felt by many boys for their mother's brothers; and there is a sexual relationship between fathers and mothers (of which children doubtless become aware at an earlier age than in most Western societies) which does not result in the development of hostile feelings directed from son to father. If there are universal feelings of antipathy between boys and *some* adult males involved in *some* kind of interpersonal relationship with the boys' mothers—and there is evidence that *this* may perhaps be true[14]—the source of that antipathy will have to be found in something other than sexual jealousy.[15]

As to the possibility that adult personality patterns and characteristics grow out of a repressed Oedipus complex, there simply is no direct evidence available that meets any empirical criteria.

* * *

The concept of the ego defense mechanism is central to all psychoanalytic theory. The defense mechanism can take a variety of forms; repression, denial, projection, sublimation, and displacement are the forms most commonly encountered in psychoanalytic literature. So little empirical support has been found for denial and projection, although they are still heavily used by psychoanalytic writers, that even as sympathetic a reviewer as Paul Kline, (whose work is an acknowledged effort to "put psychoanalysis back among the sciences") admits that there has been no objective verification of the existence of these mechanisms. He concedes that little better can be said for the concept of sublimation. Displacement, on the other hand, has been rather well confirmed, at least in terms of superficial manifestation, and is widely regarded as a major force behind anti-Semitic and racist attitudes.[16] Displacement is the well-known process of redirecting aggressive feelings away from a threatening source and toward a more acceptable one; the salesman who becomes unwarrantably angry with a subordinate after a difficult time with a client would be a common example.

Defense mechanisms are conventionally divided between successful and unsuccessful defenses—between those which find an outlet and those which do not. The most important and frequently noted of the unsuccessful defenses is repression. Repression essentially involves the exclusion from consciousness of painful material such as memories, emotions, or desires. Such material is, in a sense, pushed back into the unconscious, or so it is hypothesized, and does not then exist as far as the conscious mind is concerned. What makes repression so important to psychoanalysis is that, although the conscious mind is unaware of the existence of the repressed material, such material does not fail to exert influence on behavior. On the contrary, as with the Oedipal hypothesis, psychoanalysis sees repression as a major unconscious influence on behavior.

Needless to say, obtaining objective verification of the mechanism of repression is far from simple. The most frequently used investigative method for many years was the attempt to measure emotional responses, through various covert techniques, to "emotive" and "neutral" words. Recognition thresholds were computed, on the assumption that emotive or "taboo" words will show a higher emotional recognition threshold than neutral words if the mechanism of repression really exists. Another similar technique was to flash on a screen sentences of both neutral and "repressible" content—especially sexual and hostile parental impulses—and then to test for recall, on the assumption that if repression exists recall will be higher for the neutral sentences. Most such studies did indeed confirm the most superficial aspects of the repression hypothesis, but the design problems of such studies were obviously manifold. Other experimenters, for instance, repeatedly showed that outside factors, such as general familiarity with the words presented and whether or not preliminary instructions had created an expectation of taboo words or forbidden ideas, greatly affected the experimental results. The positive results of these early tests are still taken seriously by some, but the central critical problems have changed only in degree since Leo Postman and Gerald S. Blum raised them in an exchange in the *Journal of Abnormal and Social Psychology* in the mid-1950s.[17]

Most recent work on repression has been considerably more sophisticated—and has consistently failed to support the psychoanalytic hypothesis. It is important to emphasize here that these varied studies have *not* concluded that, as one survey puts it, "there is no selectivity in what persons are able to report of their previous experiences," but rather that "the patterning of the selectivity is often inconsistent with the predictions derived from the theory of repression, and/or the findings can be better accounted for by processes other than repression."[18] The most generous currently-held scientific opinion on the concept of repression—the concept that Freud himself termed "the cornerstone on which the whole structure of psychoanalysis rests"[19]—is aptly summed-up by psychologist David S. Holmes:

> Clearly, it appears that either new research must be conducted which will support the concept of repression, or

the concept of repression must be discarded and the variety of concepts related to or dependent upon the concept
of repression will have to be reevaluated or reinterpreted.
In view of the amount and consistency of the data accumulated to this point, and pending new data supporting the
concept of repression, the continued use of repression as
an explanation for behavior does not seem justifiable.[20]

As for the entire range of psychoanalytic hypotheses concerning
the so-called defense mechanisms, what we now know with any
assurance is only that people often do not admit into their everyday
thinking unpleasant or uncomfortable memories, emotions, or desires, and that people often focus their aggressions on objects less
threatening than those which inspired the aggression. But that,
really, is about all we know—and I shall leave it to others to decide
whether or not pre-Freudian common sense wisdom might not have
made the same deductions. The crucial point, however, is that the
psychoanalytic web that has been spun about these phenomena is,
after all these years, still nothing more than speculation—and
speculation that is directly contrary to the findings of a now
enormous body of scientific research.

*　　　*　　　*

The psychoanalytic theory of psychosexual personality syndromes
has been of major importance to those historians who use psychoanalytic concepts in their constructions of historical explanation. A
division is customarily made by psychoanalysts between the so-
called pregenital characteristics, those referred to as oral and anal,
and another set known as urethral and phallic—these latter two
initially suggested by Ernest Jones. There is, it can be flatly stated,
no empirical evidence for the so-called urethral and phallic personality constellations; they have been largely ignored by psychohistorians and are not even very important in recent psychoanalytic
theory.[21]

The hypothesis that there are constellations of personality traits derived from repressed oral and anal erotism is, however, of great importance to psychoanalytic theory, has been of much use to psychohistorical explanation, and has considerable potential for confirmation by objective testing. In brief, Freud's theory of psychosexual personality patterns postulates that "it is an untenable error to deny that children have a sexual life and to suppose that sexuality only begins at puberty with the maturation of the genitals. On the contrary, from the very first children have a copious sexual life, which differs at many points from what is later regarded as normal."[22] The initial stage of childhood differing from normal adult sexuality appears during the first year of life and involves a concentration on oral satisfaction. Either excessive or inadequate satisfaction can allegedly produce a fixation on the oral stage of infantile sexuality, and through the process of reaction-formation or sublimation this fixation may appear in an adult personality pattern characterized by ambition, envy, and impatience. There are many other traits often alleged to be part of the oral character, but they are most often subsumed under this famous triad.

Beginning around the middle of the second year and extending until the ages of four to five, the second phase of psychosexual development—the anal phase—is said to appear. Most psychoanalysts since Anna Freud, however, accept the probability of overlap between all stages of infant sexuality. The timing and rigidity of toilet training, among other factors, may, it is claimed, produce fixation on this stage of sexuality, which will be expressed in an adult character marked by the traits of frugality, obstinacy, and orderliness. Again, as with the oral character, this triad is only a summary of a great many more specific traits, such as attention to detail and a desire to dominate.

The first and most direct way of testing these psychoanalytic hypotheses is to attempt to determine if the traits in question do in fact tend to cluster in individual personalities. Because, once again, clinical evidence based on individual cases is inevitably fraught with problems of bias, what is required for this sort of investigation are large-scale studies, preferably of both "normal" and "abnormal" populations.

The first of two large studies on the oral character conducted by Frieda Goldman and published in *The Journal of Personality* focused on the presence of oral trait clustering in a normal sample of 115 adults in London. Analytic questionnaires were administered that sought information on the subjects' behavior in given situations rather than their self-evaluations, an important improvement over previous studies. The oral character is said to be generally manifested in two patterns known as oral optimist and oral pessimist—once again introducing the ever-present problem of irrefutability. Nevertheless, tentative confirmation that most of the hypothesized traits were clustered among a significant proportion of the sample led Goldman to conclude that there is empirical support for the thesis that character traits corresponding to the psychoanalytic oral character types do tend to occur in certain personality constellations.[23]

Certain problems in Goldman's study, such as the relative homogeneity and limited size of her sample and the fact that she used a rather loose interpretation of traits described as oral, were reduced in a subsequent study by Charles A. Barnes that examined the entire theory of psychosexual development. A larger, somewhat more heterogeneous sample was analyzed, and greater specificity was given the traits sought. Barnes' findings were quite contrary to Goldman's: there was some suggestion that certain traits clustered, but these were too insubstantial to support the psychoanalytic hypotheses.[24]

A third and still more recent study by A. Lazare, which also sought confirmation of the entire theory of psychosexual development, concentrated on ninety female subjects who had previously been diagnosed as neurotic. The traits sought were the same as those sought in Goldman's work. The results showed tentative support for the oral personality syndrome.[25]

The citing of such studies could continue at some length, but conclusions to date remain contradictory. There appears to be *some* empirical support for the contention that personality traits tend to cluster in a way suggested by the psychoanalytic concept of the oral character. That some sophisticated studies have failed to find a significant correlation among these personality traits, however, strongly suggests that the concept is either very weak or severely limited in applicability.

The existence of a personality constellation resembling that of the psychoanalytic anal character has more support than does the oral hypothesis. The study by Barnes, though it concludes that none of the psychosexual personality syndromes receives adequate support, does at least show a higher tendency for traits of an anal nature to cluster. Lazare's study of female neurotics shows overall support for the psychoanalytic hypotheses and greater support for the anal than the oral character. A 1957 study of school-age subjects by Halla Beloff in Northern Ireland further showed support for the existence of a personality type resembling that characterized by psychoanalytic theory as anal, though no support was shown for a relationship between this personality type and any particular type of toilet training experience.[26]

A final study worth mentioning is one carried out by Paul Kline in Ghana in 1969. An exceptionally careful analysis of a Ghanaian student population showed a marked tendency for the so-called anal traits to cluster, and a comparative study of British students indicated a relatively higher incidence of that pattern's occurrence among the Ghanaians. Apart from its statistical significance, this study is worthy of note because of its revelation of the personality syndrome among a non-American and non-British population, the sources of almost every other important study.[27]

In summary, then, it seems safe to say that the psychoanalytic hypothesis that certain personality traits tend to cluster—specifically the so-called anal traits of frugality, obstinacy, and orderliness—receives some confirmation from empirical investigation.

The clustering of oral traits is considerably more problematic than that of anal traits, but the negative evidence, though strong, is not conclusive. It is essential, however, to stress the limited meaning of these research findings. All that these studies have shown is that if an individual has a tendency to be frugal, obstinate, *or* orderly, there is a fairly significant likelihood that he or she will also have a tendency to display the remaining two traits. There is a potential, but lesser, likelihood that if an individual has a tendency to be either ambitious, envious, *or* impatient, he or she may also have a tendency to display the remaining two traits. The possibility that most people who have never read a word of psychoanalytic theory would tend to make similar or identical trait associations and predictions suggests a certain banality to these findings, but Freud and his followers *did* construct the theory, and it has tended to find at least mixed support in empirical investigation. What remains to be seen is whether there is any evidence to support the claim that these personality patterns derive from childhood experiences. If they do not, the most that can be said for psychoanalytic theory in this regard is that it has provided labels—and inaccurate and misleading ones at that—for certain commonly recognized trait clusters.

*   *   *

The hypothesis that adult personality patterns and characteristics derive directly from infant and childhood experiences is so ingrained in modern thought that to question it seems almost foolish. Philosophers and others long before Freud stated and repeated the dictum that the molding of a child's attitudes meant the molding of the adult's. They generally spoke of the positive aspects of this process. Schopenhauer spoke from another perspective when he wrote: "There is no absurdity so palpable but that it may be firmly planted in the human head if only you begin to inculcate it before the age of five, by constantly repeating it with an air of great solemnity." But whatever the value placed on childhood malleability, it has long been popularly accepted as fact. To this view, Freud brought the apparatus of psychoanalysis in his attempt to transform what had become a platitude into a scientific system. With remarkable insight and imagination he constructed a complex of hypotheses that became perhaps the most celebrated concerns of psychoanalytic theory, hypotheses that themselves rested on the fundamental importance of infancy and childhood in the molding of the adult.

What remained was to test those hypotheses to see how much substance lay behind the pure ideas. If the postulated links between *specific* infant experiences and *specific* adult character patterns could be experimentally demonstrated and replicated, many of the other shortcomings of psychoanalysis (therapeutic failure and logical turbidity, for instance) might at least be overshadowed by these great discoveries. Without demonstrable evidence of this sort of causality, however, the hypotheses would remain just that—imaginative constructs, not unlike those of astrology: complex, vague, logically circular, intermittently accurate (the result of chance and/or suggestion), and of scholarly interest primarily to the historian of strange ideas.

We have seen that the psychoanalytic view is that certain adult character patterns derive in large measure from early or late weaning and its severity, early or late and rigid or flexible toilet training, and the nature and duration of affection or antipathy for each of one's parents. Certainly children do undergo a variety of experiences regarding each of these matters; and certainly there are people who exhibit the personality clusters psychoanalytically labeled oral-erotic, anal-erotic, and—to mention one to be discussed later—paranoid schizophrenic. The question that is crucial, however, remains: is it empirically demonstrable that these childhood experiences do actually produce or even significantly contribute to the character types described?

A great deal of research has been devoted to this question. All attempts to validate the hypotheses, however, have been beset from the start with a basic and almost insurmountable methodological problem: how to establish accurate information concerning the specific childhood experiences *and* specific adult personality patterns of a sizable body of individuals. Psychoanalytic sources of such information—the selective and highly questionable infant and childhood memories of patients under care—are totally unacceptable to the researcher seeking confirmation or disconfirmation of the theory, since even parents' memories concerning dates of weaning and toilet training have been shown to be seriously inaccurate after as short an interval as one year.

One rather comprehensive study which artificially inflated the probability of accurate parental recall asked participating parents to submit progress reports both in writing and in person throughout their children's infancy. The study tested parental recall when the children were only three years old and found common inaccuracies of as much as six months (an enormous discrepancy in discussing just two to three years of life) in remembered dates of weaning, the onset and conclusion of bowel training, and other milestones of infancy. Only slightly more than one-third of the fathers and one-half of the mothers questioned remembered accurately whether the child had been fed on a schedule or on a demand basis, and—in striking support of the idea that suggestion is an ever-present problem—almost all of the distortions tended to be in the direction of the schedule recommendations contained in Benjamin Spock's *Baby and Child Care.* The sample of parents studied was, as a group, highly educated, and—of great importance—*they were aware that their memories would be checked against the records they themselves had prepared.*[28]

Needless to say, evidence of this sort casts serious doubt on the accuracy of psychoanalytic patient recall and on studies relying on parental recollection of childhood training, experiences, and events. Thus, the substantial body of studies that employ parental recall in gathering infant training data must at best be treated with great caution. Nevertheless, it is at least worth noting that since the first such studies of any size or complexity were conducted in the 1930s, there has to date been only *one* of any sophistication that has found even tentative support for any psychoanalytically hypothesized links between specific infant care and specific adult personality patterns. And this study flatly contradicts other parts of the orality hypothesis.[29] That research has so consistently resulted in negative findings does not, of course, reduce the significance of possible flaws in the research design, but neither should these findings be totally ignored.

An improvement on the retrospective types of investigation are the types known as current and longitudinal. Current and longitudinal studies seek direct confirmation of childhood training procedures, either by interview, questionnaire, observation, or a combination of these measures. These studies, however, are not without problems of their own. While the data on infancy and childhood successfully deal with the problem of veracity, many of these studies have plotted these data against personality patterns apparent only in pre-pubertal children. The psychoanalyst's objection here is obvious: repression is said to be most successful during the pre-pubertal or "latency" stage of development, so it is only natural that the predicted personality syndromes will not be evident. This is a legitimate objection, at least so long as one accepts the concept of repression. Nonetheless, it is understandable why the psychoanalyst is quick to raise it: not a single current or longitudinal study of reasonable size or sophistication has shown any links between childhood training and subsequent personality.[30]

The one study that best addresses the problems inherent in both the retrospective and longitudinal techniques was reported on by M. I. Hernstein in 1963. Hernstein maintained careful records of the type and duration of infant feeding experiences for close to 100 children, evenly divided by sex. He then followed his subjects' progress into adulthood, noting any overt displays of personality problems and administering various psychological tests of personality development to all the subjects at ages twelve and eighteen. None of the evidence, at any point, supported the hypothesis that infant feeding experiences have an effect on subsequent personality.[31]

Most recently, in a comprehensive 1979 review of research to date on the etiology of the so-called anal character, Jerrold M. Pollak has shown that "there is little, if any, empirical evidence for the classical psychoanalytic position on the etiology of the obsessive-compulsive or anal character type," further noting (as had others before him) that what little positive evidence there is can be more readily correlated with an *overall* style of long-term parental influence, rather than specific toilet training practices.[32]

There is little need to go on. The conclusions of *all* these studies overwhelmingly indicate that the specific links psychoanalytic theory alleges to exist between infant care and adult personality are little more than imaginary. This judgment appears to be so contrary to what is popularly considered fact (a condition, to borrow Schopenhauer's words, probably resulting from decades of repeating the alleged truism "with an air of great solemnity") that objections arise immediately. Paul Kline asserts that failure of confirmation is due to deficiencies in research design; we must reserve judgment, he says, until superior testing techniques are devised. This same objection is posed from another perspective by Anthony F. C. Wallace, who thinks the reason that empirical investigation has failed in its efforts to confirm psychoanalytic theory is rooted in the labyrinthian intricacies of that theory: "they are so fantastically complex and so protracted that empirical observation cannot record a sufficient number of relevant dimensions."[33]

All of this may be so. But the fact is that dozens of sophisticated independent investigations of the relationship between infant experience and adult personality have repeatedly failed to find *any* significant support for psychoanalytic theory in this regard. If there are design difficulties in these investigations, there is, of course, good reason to treat their conclusions with care. But it simply will not do to denounce them and proceed to act, without any supporting evidence, as though the psychoanalytic hypotheses were *true*. To take this position is to mimic the religious zealot whose faith in the spirits remains unshaken by the repeated failures of his or her mystical predictions—an individual, by the way, whose "pathological" behavior has been of great interest to Freud and his followers.

The unavoidable conclusion is clear: given the present and not inconsiderable state of scientific knowledge, there is *no support* for the psychoanalytic hypotheses that relate personality syndromes to specific aspects of infant care and experience. The results of dozens of investigations are virtually unanimous on this point. "As a set of hypotheses [psychoanalysis] was a great achievement fifty years ago," observed the philosopher Michael Scriven in 1959, but "as no more than a set of hypotheses it is a great disgrace today."[34] That was twenty years ago. Harsh though Scriven's judgment may sound, there is even more reason to hold to it now. To escape that judgment, more than rhetorical flourishes concerning inadequate test design are required; after all, *the burden of positive proof rests with the psychoanalyst*. To many, however, such a long and complete record of failure is now sufficient: "The original psychoanalytic variables of interest—duration of nursing, severity of weaning, and age of toilet training—are no longer of interest today." So writes Jerome Kagan, widely regarded by psychologists as the foremost living expert on early childhood.[35]

This conclusion does not mean, of course, that childhood experiences are irrelevant: it means that *psychoanalytic* theory regarding those experiences is empirically unsupportable. Post-Freudian modifications of orthodox theory by such writers as Horney, Fromm, Sullivan, Erikson and others have attempted to appear more closely aligned with certain of the empirical findings; but these modifications have been slight, have too often been politically motivated and sociologically naïve, and—most important—have not themselves been the subject of rigorous, empirical examination.[36]

This conclusion also does not mean—and this is a point deserving emphasis—that a great deal of non-psychoanalytic psychological research on the importance of childhood should be denigrated, although (and this too deserves emphasis) the best recent work now suggests that the popularly presumed effects of *any* infant experiences on subsequent personality have been vastly overrated.[37] All that is specifically affected by the research discussed above is psychoanalytic theory. Unfortunately, however, it is psychoanalytic theory that has provided the psychohistorians with their models.

*   *   *

So far we have reviewed the empirical status of the Oedipus complex, repression, the anal and oral personality syndromes, and the importance to adult personality of infant care and experience. Although in certain cases, disconfirmation of one psychoanalytic hypothesis, either by logical or empirical criteria, clearly implies *de facto* disconfirmation of other hypotheses dependent upon the first, I have avoided employing this kind of domino theory approach. Each hypothesis has been regarded as employing acceptable primary assumptions, whether or not those assumptions were shown elsewhere to be untenable, in order to test the hypothesis in its strongest state. Before proceeding further, it seems worthwhile to recapitulate these earlier findings.

It has been seen that there is some empirical support for the thesis that in a number of cultures male children may develop a rather early sense of antipathy for a certain adult male involved in a close relationship with the child's mother. In the West this attitude, when it appears, is generally directed at the boy's father, but this is not necessarily the case in every culture—and even in the West its degree of conventionality remains a matter of debate. There is virtually no support for the contention that this antipathy is founded on sexual jealousy, although if "sexual" is defined broadly enough some meager support might be found. There is some support for the thesis that when this antipathy exists it can persist at least into puberty, but that often it is not readily confessed to by the child. Whether this is due to repression (and the emotion is thus not conscious) or merely social pressure is as yet unknown. What has never been demonstrated, however, is that these childhood emotions have any effect whatever on adult personality. If, simply on the basis of common sense, we were to reject the best recent findings and assume that these childhood emotions must have *some* impact on adult character, we must conclude that one person's guess is as good as any other's concerning the nature of that impact. There is simply no empirical evidence to go on.

We have seen that of the psychoanalytic mechanisms of defense, only displacement has to any extent at all weathered the rigors of empirical investigation. Repression, by far the most important defense, has been shown to exist only if it is defined merely as the tendency to forget or otherwise not admit into everyday thought unpleasant or uncomfortable memories, emotions, or desires. The belief that such matters are secretly lurking in a place known as the unconscious has been seen as logically untenable, and there is also no empirical evidence concerning the systematic effects of repression on behavior or personality. If, as with the so-called Oedipus complex, we assume that such forgotten matter might have *some* influence on personality, the nature of that influence remains unknown.

We have seen that the personality trait constellations labeled by psychoanalytic theory as oral and anal do sometimes find tentative, partial support in empirical investigation. That is, the traits of frugality, obstinancy, and orderliness may tend to appear together in certain individual personalities; to a lesser, but still possibly significant extent, the traits of ambition, envy, and impatience also may cluster in certain individuals. This is a fairly trivial discovery, however—at least in terms of verifying psychoanalytic theory—unless support is also shown for the contention that such personality syndromes have their roots in specific experiences of infancy and childhood.

We have seen that the virtually unanimous conclusion of dozens

of empirical studies over the past few decades has been that there is
no discernable link between specific child-rearing practices and
adult personality patterns as postulated by psychoanalytic theory.
No doubt some childhood experiences do influence subsequent personality characteristics, particularly when those experiences are of a
profound and enduring nature. Depression, for example, appears to
have a disproportionately high rate of occurrence among individuals who were orphaned during early adolescence, and other empirically verified connections between childhood experience and adult
personity can be found in the literature of experimental psychology.[38] The crucial point in this discussion, however, is that the
most fundamental *psychoanalytic* hypotheses concerning such relationships have repeatedly failed to find empirical support.

For the purposes of the historian, then, the value of psychoanalytic theory appears largely limited to its providing a kind of shorthand for superficially *describing* observable behavior that otherwise
would require more detailed and complex verbal elaboration. Thus,
historians Richard Hofstadter and David Brion Davis once found
"paranoid style" a convenient way of labeling social attitudes that are
laden with conspiratorial imagery, though they both cautioned that
they were not speaking of the "disease of paranoia." The paranoid
style as they defined it "has to do with the way in which ideas are
believed and advocated rather than with the truth or falsity of their
content."[39] Even with this caution, however, reviewers of their work
often ignored the caveat and upbraided them for failing to distin-
guish between the "truth or falsity" of the conspiratorial frame of
mind.[40] Since Hofstadter and Davis both seemed to be using the term
only in an effort to achieve incisiveness in communication, and since
they both seem to have been widely misunderstood, it might be
prudent for historians in the future to think twice before following
their lead.

Other historians have been far less judicious in their use of paranoia as an explanatory term. Bruce Mazlish, for instance, calls

Richard Nixon's fervid anti-communism during the 1950s and early 1960s evidence of "paranoid fear" (an affliction, Mazlish fails to note, shared by millions of Americans other than Nixon and one from which Nixon apparently recovered during his first term in office).[41] Psychohistorical work on Hitler has, of course, been riddled with such references. But as Mazlish and other psychoanalytically informed historians well know, paranoia is a phenomenon that in the psychoanalytic lexicon has a specific meaning with specific antecedent causes. The most fundamental cause, discussed at length initially in Freud's analysis of Dr. Schreber, is the projection of homosexual desires. The formula, as Freud explicated it is: "I (a man) *love him* (a man)." Since this emotion is unacceptable, it takes the form of a reaction-formation against homosexuality and becomes: "I do not *love* him—I *hate* him." The explication continues:

> This contradiction, which must have run thus in the unconscious, cannot, however, become conscious to a paranoic in this form. The mechanism of symptom-formation in paranoia requires that internal perceptions—feelings—shall be replaced by external perceptions. Consequently the proposition "I hate him" becomes transformed by *projection* into another one: *"He hates* (persecutes) *me,* which will justify me in hating him." And thus the impelling unconscious feeling makes its appearance as though it were the consequence of an external perception: "I do not *love* him—I *hate* him, because HE PERSECUTES ME."[42]

If Mazlish and others who use paranoia as an explanation for behavior are not merely indulging in hyperbole for literary effect (as I suspect they are not), and if they are not merely echoing Hofstadter and Davis without their disclaimers (as I also suspect they are not), they must be able to historically justify their selection of such highly specific clinical language—unless, of course, there is no empirical evidence to support the connection between repressed and projected homosexuality and paranoid behavior. Should this turn out to be the case, their analytical language is necessarily reduced to metaphor.

A good deal of research, both clinical and experimental, has been conducted on the psychoanalytic hypothesis linking paranoia and repressed homosexuality. The results have been mixed. At least as many studies have failed to support the theory as have claimed to verify it, and a good many others have admitted substantial ambiguity in their findings. Since it is impossible to review here all the relevant major studies, it seems most appropriate to at least examine the two works that have been hailed by proponents of psychoanalysis as providing the strongest support for the theory. For, whatever the strengths or weaknesses of the contradictory studies, the most minimal requirement for even tentatively accepting the psychoanalytic hypothesis is that its strongest empirical support should withstand general scrutiny.

In a study published in 1956, P. G. Daston submitted seventy-five subjects—twenty-five "normal," twenty-five diagnosed as nonparanoid schizophrenics, and twenty-five diagnosed as paranoid—to a word recognition test with the aid of a tachistoscope (a device commonly used in psychological research that exposes visual stimuli for extremely brief periods, often a tenth of a second or less). The words flashed varied widely in reference and emotional content, but a number of words with clear homosexual reference were included among them. As hypothesized, the group diagnosed as paranoid showed a superior ability to identify the homosexual words than did either of the other two nonparanoid groups. Daston concluded that this outcome indicated support for at least this one aspect of the psychoanalytic hypothesis.[43]

Two years following Daston's report, H. S. Zamansky published the results of a similar but more complex study. Zamansky selected twenty paranoid and twenty nonparanoid hospitalized psychotics and showed them pictures in pairs, one of which depicted a male and one of which depicted a female. Some pictures in each case depicted the subjects in positions suggestive of homosexuality. Since previous study had shown that homosexuals spend more time looking at male than at female pictures, Zamansky hypothesized on the basis of psychoanalytic theory that the paranoids in his study would also spend more time looking at male than at female pictures *and* that their time so spent would exceed that spent by the nonparanoid (but still psychotic) subjects. Zamansky then added a second intriguing hypothesis: if psychoanalytic theory regarding repression of the homosexual impulses were correct, paranoids would *acknowledge* their preference of male over female to a lesser degree than was indicated by their selective viewing time of the pictures, and the degree of difference between acknowledged and unacknowledged preference would be greater than that for the nonparanoid subjects. Both of these hypotheses were supported by Zamansky's experiment.[44]

But did these studies actually confirm the psychoanalytic hypothesis? Even if all the studies with contradictory conclusions are discounted, what Daston and Zamansky found was that in a specific cultural setting (the Midwestern and Northeastern United States in the early and mid-1950s) the appearance of homosexual impulses occurred more frequently in a population diagnosed as paranoid than in populations not regarded as paranoid. Zamansky added the further observation that "men with paranoid delusions tend to avoid explicit or direct manifestation of homosexual object preference."[45] This is a long way indeed from psychoanalytic theory, which posits a *causal* connection between repressed homosexuality and paranoia. Both the relatively small sample sizes and the fact that only a slightly higher degree of apparent homosexuality was observed among the paranoid subjects than among the control groups suggest the possibility that factors not considered may have been responsible for the discrepancy; after all, no matter how a population of such limited size is divided, some characteristics (physical as well as psychological) will invariably occur more frequently in one group than in another. Even if we disregard this obvious shortcoming, however, we are still left without *any* evidence of causation. Forget for the moment any and all internal problems with these studies. Accept without question the claim that there *is* a correlation between homosexual tendencies and paranoid behavior. We still have no way of knowing if this correlation is due to a causal link between the two entities (in one direction or another) or if *both* entities are independently caused by a third factor.

As to Zamansky's finding that a covert method of testing for homosexuality resulted in a higher proportion of discovered individuals with homosexual tendencies than did an overt method of testing, that is what anyone would logically predict. In a culture that regards homosexuality unfavorably, it is only reasonable to expect a certain amount of concealment. There is no need, and no justification, for regarding the discrepancy between overt and covert results as evidence of repression unless there is evidence to indicate that no conscious deception was involved in the subjects' replies to direct questions. And no such evidence exists. Neither is it a surprise that the discrepancy between the overt and covert tests was higher for the paranoid group than for the nonparanoid group. After all, if we accept the initial findings, the paranoid group had the most to conceal in that it showed in the covert test a higher tendency toward homosexuality than did the nonparanoid group—a difference, in fact, somewhat higher than that measured for the overt/covert discrepancy.

Even this is excessively generous. These two studies are generally regarded as the strongest empirical support available for the psychoanalytic thesis concerning repressed homosexuality and paranoia (though the researchers themselves are more circumspect in their claims).[46] What they show is interesting, but limited. They *suggest* that in a specific cultural setting men who have been diagnosed as paranoid schizophrenics will probably spend more time than will nonparanoid schizophrenics in looking at pictures of men, particularly men who may be homosexual, than at pictures of women. In the earlier study, men who have been diagnosed as paranoid appear to be more responsive than do nonparanoid schizophrenics to words charged with homosexual meaning. Well, of course they do. Paranoid people are, after all, by definition especially suspicious of and alert to anything that may be regarded as threatening. And men, particularly sexually "deviant" men, may well appear more threatening than women. Why do the diagnosed paranoids not acknowledge their apparent preference as readily as do the nonparanoids? The most obvious reason, again, provides the most likely explanation: *because* they are *paranoid*. As paranoids they would, of course, quickly interpret the overt suggestion as threatening and deny it, whereas the nonparanoid schizophrenics would by definition be less likely to behave in *any* systematic fashion. In short, all that these two studies clearly show is that paranoids appear to act more paranoid than do nonparanoids.

Nevertheless, even if the studies are accepted without scrutiny, the most that they indicate is that there appears to be a minor statistical probability that homosexual tendencies will occur more frequently among individuals diagnosed as paranoid than among nonparanoids. Zamansky's study adds the claim that paranoids with apparent homosexual leanings are not always willing to admit them openly, or to provide obvious clues to the existence of the tendency. Even examined in the most uncritical light possible, these studies provide *no* evidence of any *causal* relationship, one way or another, between homosexuality and paranoia, nor do they provide any evidence for the existence of the mechanism of repression. In short, they do not support the psychoanalytic hypothesis and thus join in their failure at confirmation other, larger, more recent studies that flatly disconfirm psychoanalytic conjecture.[47]

Since the psychoanalytic explanation of the origins of paranoia is not supported by empirical investigation of the theory, it might be suggested that, paradoxically, the psychohistorian is thus freed to use the concept of paranoia more loosely than ever in historical explanation. There is, for example, no need for the psychohistorian to produce evidence of a subject's repressed homosexuality to justify a reference to that subject's "paranoid fears," since there is no evidence to support the psychoanalytic contention that one is antecedent to the other. On the other hand, the psychohistorian is left with a concept—paranoia—that is virtually bereft of any except very general and colloquial meaning as a label for behavior he or she regards as motivated by unrealistic feelings of persecution. The most that can be said for its use in this fashion (though the critics of Hofstadter and Davis would probably not accept even this generosity) is that as an informal label it is relatively innocuous. That is not exactly an achievement calling for celebration.

*   *   *

It must be acknowledged, before closing this chapter, that some supporters of psychohistorical analysis are quite aware of the abysmal record of psychoanalytic theory when it is subjected to logical scrutiny and empirical research. Their response has been to try to immunize their work from the consequences of such failure by stressing a radically endopsychic view of the psychoanalytic endeavor. This is the view, espoused by the French philosopher Paul Ricoeur, that frankly admits that as long as psychoanalysis is held to the same logical and empirical standards "as other theories in the natural or social sciences" the sort of criticism reviewed in the past three chapters is "unanswerable." However, Ricoeur goes on, psychoanalysis should not be held to these standards because it "is not a science of observation; it is an interpretation." What this means, he claims, is that the nature of a subject's empirically verifiable life *experiences* are irrelevant to psychoanalysis. Instead, "what is important to the analyst are the dimensions of the environment as '*believed*' by the subject; what is pertinent to him is not the fact, but the meaning the fact has assumed in the subject's history." Such beliefs and meanings, of course, are said to be buried in the unconscious and, in the words of historian Christopher Lasch, who appears to be a supporter of this general view, "have been so ruthlessly repressed that they can be brought to light only with the greatest difficulty." Thus, what matters is not whether a given individual actually experienced certain events that influenced his or her subsequent life history (the analysis of which is then subject to recognized logical and empirical examination), but whether—deeply repressed in his or her unconscious—an individual has given certain unique and behaviorally consequential *meanings* to phenomena which may in fact be wholy imaginary (a view which makes utterly irrelevant actual life experience and the individual's interaction with others). Solipsism thus becomes the final defense of a psychological theory that consistently has failed to weather the rigors of experimental verification.

The implications of this position for psychoanalysis are troubling enough, but for *psychohistory* they are nothing short of devastating. For in trying to use this argument to speciously extricate psychoanalytic theory from the effects of logical failure and experimental disconfirmation, thus hoping to free it for acceptable use as a method of historical explanation, Lasch and the others who follow this approach are caught in the trap laid by the psychoanalysts themselves: that is, that only deep, prolonged, and face-to-face personal encounters with a subject—encounters involving, writes famed analyst Heinz Hartmann, the psychoanalytic "gathering of data" not only on the subject's "verbal behavior," but also "his silences, his postures, and his movements in general, more specifically his expressive movements"—can even *hope* to reveal in a completed and successful analysis (a very rare bird, as we have seen) the "ruthlessly repressed" and extremely subjective individual interpretations that are allegedly the motives underlying a particular condition. In sum, either historically verifiable life experiences (Luther's relationship with his parents, Jackson's absence of a father, and the like) *are* relevant—in which case the theory which claims to analyze them *is* subject to the sort of logical scrutiny and empirical examination which, even Ricoeur admits, it cannot withstand; or, such experiences are not relevant, except in terms of their repressed and individually unique "meanings" the nature of which can *only* be revealed by a prolonged and therapeutically successful period of direct psychoanalytic contact with a *living* and fully cooperative individual. In either case, by either criterion, psychohistory is readily shown to be both a historical and a psychological sham. And the psychohistorian becomes (to paraphrase a remark once made by R. D. Laing) an individual hunting a hare whose tracks exist only in the mind of the hunter.[48]

5

"The past is a foreign country;
they do things differently there."

—L. P. Hartley,
The Go-Between

The Problem
of Culture

AT one point in his widely and justifiably admired study of family life in Plymouth Colony, John Demos ingeniously unites two independent observations—"the few recorded cases of conflict within a family, and the very many such cases among neighbors"— to form what he calls "the germ of an hypothesis": cramped living conditions, which created frequent "occasions for abrasive contact" within the family situation, combined with a countering force—the need for the family "to maintain a smooth kind of operational equilibrium"—to cause a displacement of hostility from family members to neighbors. Thus, Demos suggests, "a man cursed his neighbor in order to keep smiling at his parent, spouse, or child."[1]

This fascinating insight, if accurate, could shed a great deal of needed light on seventeenth-century colonial American behavior. It is, however, unsteadily dependent on a single, questionable assumption—that the settlers of Plymouth did have to endure the hardship of cramped living conditions. What, after all, *constitutes* cramped living conditions? It would be belaboring the obvious to point out that living space varies so much from society to society and from individual situation to individual situation within all societies that hard and fast formulae defining the nature of inadequate conditions would be hard to come by. True, ethologists have for some time been studying this problem with animal experiments (the overall results of which are not, by the way, supportive of the hypothesis Demos extends), but nothing resembling verifiable data yet exists for human populations in general.[2] If the Plymouth settlers' housing was sufficiently confining to produce the behavior Demos suggests, confirmation must be sought in the records and diaries and literary remains of the colonists themselves. Since Demos is an expert on this material (and since we may expect at least some of it to be covertly expressed) we might turn to him for this information.

All Demos has to say on the settlers' own reactions to their housing conditions is that to *his* eye and to that of modern students of architecture the homes of the early colonists *seem* "oppressive" to the extent that "many settlers *ought* to have looked on their homes as 'decidedly substandard.'" But the settlers themselves apparently did not share this opinion; "they did not especially complain" about their living conditions, Demos admits, and "were presumably quite content with such houses."[3]

Demos's reasoning on this matter is a classic example of the sort of historical presentism that appears to be an inevitable accompaniment of even the best psychohistorical explanations. The colonists' recorded reactions to their situation are completely ignored in forming the explanation, and an assumption is inserted in their place based on the criteria of the historical present. "Can we picture ourselves in such a setting?" Demos asks rhetorically at one point, assured of the modern reader's negative reply.[4] The modern reader would also undoubtedly reply in the negative if asked whether he or she could picture himself or herself in a setting so bereft of the benefits of modern hygiene—and one can readily imagine the provocative hypotheses that might be advanced on the premise that the Plymouth settlers constantly felt *dirty*, because they were, all moderns would agree, decidedly unclean.

If this picture seems perhaps overdrawn (though I am by no means sure most psychohistorians would consider it to be), I hope it is at least clear.* The psychohistorian employs theoretical models and cognitive assumptions created from the material of the present—and then imposes them on the past. In so doing, he or she must assume that in most fundamental ways all people, at all places, at all times, have viewed themselves and the world about them in substantially the same fashion. If man *qua* man were not always essentially the same, the behavior of many past individuals (to say nothing of whole cultures) would be psychoanalytically unintelligible. Their actions and motives would be operating at a level beyond the reach of psychoanalytic concepts and suppositions, which are products of the direct study of primarily urban, post-industrial, literate, twentieth-century, Western individuals—and mostly "abnormal" and demographically non-representative ones at that.

The assumption of immutability in man's basic vision of himself and his environment has, of course, been sharply challenged. While not always addressing directly the then still exotic vogue of psychoanalysis, such great early twentieth-century historians as Huizinga and Febvre (who were by no means always in agreement with one another) both implicitly and explicitly suggested that the historical past was in *fundamental* ways a very different world from that of the present. More recently, a historian of the Middle Ages, D. W. Robertson, Jr., has argued that the people of medieval London were devoid of "something that most of us enjoy today: 'personality.'" Instead, he contends, medieval men "thought of one another . . . as moral characters whose virtues or vices were apparent in their speech and actions"; as a result, "the less inclined we are to think of medieval

---

*By "most psychohistorians" I am not here including Demos who, despite the logical gaffe I have pointed to, is a cautious, skilled, and sensitive historian.

men sentimentally as being 'human like ourselves' the more fruitful will be our study of the medieval city and its people." Psychoanalyst J. H. van den Berg argues similarly and eloquently that his profession is disastrously wedded to the mistaken assumption of psychic uniformity in time and place. Psychologist Bernard G. Rosenthal warns of the "scientific provincialism" such assumptions imply. And in his pathbreaking study of the family in Western history, Philippe Ariès notes that the "lack of reserve with regard to children" observed as late as the early seventeenth century "surprises us: we raise our eyebrows at the outspoken talk but even more at the bold gestures, the physical contacts, about which it is easy to imagine what a modern psychoanalyst would say." He adds: "The psychoanalyst would be wrong."[5]

A list such as this could continue at some length, but even if extended indefinitely it would run into two serious objections. The first has been alluded to by Erik Erikson, who wrote in his epilogue to *Young Man Luther:* "I will not discuss here the cultural relativity of Freud's observations nor the dated origin of his term [the Oedipus complex]; but I assume that those who do wish to quibble about all this will feel the obligation to advance specific propositions about family, childhood and society which come closer to the core, rather than go back to the periphery of the riddle which Freud was the first to penetrate."[6] Erikson may well be engaging here in what David Hackett Fischer has called the "fallacy of the presumptive proof" and forgetting or ignoring the fact that the burden of responsibility "rests squarely upon Erikson, and not his quibbling critics, to advance specific propositions which come closer to the core."[7] But clearly Erikson does touch a nerve in his critics. If it is not their responsiblity to write better psychoanalytic theory, it does at least seem incumbent upon them to show that their quibbling has empirical support and is not merely founded on the *suspicion* that cultural differences are sufficient to blunt the validity of psychohistorical explanation.

The second objection is more philosophical and speculative. In a sense it is the reverse of Erickson's critique. What if the critics of the immutability assumption are right? Where does it end? As Hans Jonas has pointed out:

> . . . the proposition of the irreducible uniqueness of all experience and the ever-otherness of man in history can also lead to the radically skeptical conclusion that "true" historical understanding is a priori impossible; and that what we take for it is always a translation of the foreign signs into our own language—a necessarily falsifying translation, which creates the deceptive appearance of familiarity where in fact we only explicate ourselves and can recognize ourselves in the past because we have first projected ourselves into it.[8]

Such extreme skepticism would seem to support the old arguments of Croce and Oakeshott that historical knowledge based on discovery and interpretation is impossible. It would also almost inevitably endorse the more recent "Construction Theory" of Jack W. Meiland which argues that the best a historian can do, since the past can never be known, is to "'tell a story' which is in the past tense."[9] Meiland's position, however, falls prey to the traditional rejoinder that such skepticism is not limited to history, but extends to all knowledge of others; it is most properly a general, and quite traditional, question of epistemology. Further, it is a self-defeating and eventually, at least in the eyes of most historians, meaningless position of self-reinforcing negativism. It becomes the kind of problem seemingly so removed from the world of working historians (psychohistorian and non-psychohistorian alike) that they most often, and quite properly, regard it as armchair philosophizing—and then return to the work at hand.

Clearly, if the argument is to be successfully advanced that psychohistory in its present form fails to deal with the "differentness" of distant individuals and cultures, these two objections will have to be faced. It must be demonstrated that cultural milieux can and do seriously affect the most fundamental aspects of human life and cognition; and it must be shown that some sort of generalization (if not conventional, culture-bound psychoanalysis) is still possible once the effects of cultural influence are seen.

On the other hand, if these criteria can be met, if the common psychoanalytic assumption of immutability can be shown to be false, the work of the practicing psychohistorian will have to be regarded with whatever respect would be given a physician who treated all his or her patients with superficially similar symptoms in precisely the same manner, without ever considering the possibility that the phenomena at the *source* of the symptoms may well differ from patient to patient—thus still further compounding the problem that this physician is using a method of treatment that is, in the *best* of circumstances, flagrantly illogical and incapable of weathering the most elementary tests of scientific inquiry.

The phenomenon perhaps most fundamental to, and most near the "source" of human behavior, is perception. Before an individual—or any organism, for that matter—can act, he or she must perceive the environment in which he or she is acting. The individual must acquire information and somehow "process" that information before it can be acted upon. No matter how one construes the nature of "mind," it is obvious that, as one psychologist writes, "perception is the information system of the mental apparatus."[10] Thus, the question of cultural variability in perception seems a logical place to begin an investigation of the immutability of the human condition.

*   *   *

Freud's observation, noted earlier, that the poets and philosophers long before him had discovered the unconscious, was one that might be made of the scientific "discovery" of any number of phenomena. Almost two thousand years before psychologists began inquiring into the effects of environment on perception, for example, Protagoras had pointed out that the same wind can appear cold to one person and warm to another. According to this most famous of the Sophists, in matters of perceptual disagreement there is no correct and objective answer. On the contrary, the wind that appears warm *is* warm, and the wind that appears cold *is* cold, and all perceptions are thus in a sense "true." Yet, at least according to one student of scientific thought, conventional nineteenth-century science tended to view the human mind as "an inanimate and impartial motion-picture film which accurately records the succession of physical events. It is a percept-registering or fact-registering organ with the attributes of a scientific instrument."[11]

But the poets continued to disagree. In his preface to *The Portrait of a Lady*, Henry James wrote:

> The house of fiction has in short not one window, but a million. . . . at each of them stands a figure with a pair of eyes, or at least with a field-glass, which forms, again and again, for observation, a unique instrument, insuring to the person making use of it an impression distinct from every other. He and his neighbors are watching the same show, but one seeing more where the other sees less, one seeing black where the other sees white, one seeing big where the other sees small, one seeing coarse where the other sees fine.[12]

It was not long after this that modern novelists, most notably James Joyce and William Faulkner, began expressing in detail the theme that what people see in others is to a large extent a reflection of themselves. Anthropologists, beginning with W. H. R. Rivers in 1901, started working on the implications for their investigations of the possibility that, as Levy-Bruhl wrote, "primitives perceive nothing in the same way as we do."[13] Finally, in the middle of the twentieth century psychologists and anthropologists, in a movement they called the "New Look," were working on a scientific method by which the phenomenon of relativity in perception might be studied.

It was not until the late 1940s, however, that substantial psychological and anthropological explanations were advanced concerning the phenomenon of the influence of a perceiver's cultural history on his or her perceptions.[14] Anthony F. C. Wallace later summarized the implications of this position:

> This quasi-independence of perception from the "objective" reality of nature makes possible two mental phenomena: first, the ability of the perceiver to say that two sensibly different experiences involve the "same thing" ("sameness" being determined by constancy of configuration, by continuity over time in space, or by various other criteria); second, the possibility of two perceivers, or the same observer at different times, perceiving the "same" object differently, depending on differences in their own perceptual equipment and experience.[15]

This latter phenomenon was something with which field anthropologists had long been familiar. For some years anthropologists had observed the reactions of people who had never seen a camera, to a photograph of one or another local scene. One of them, Melville Herskovits, later described and explained one such experience:

> To those of us accustomed to the idiom of the realism of the photographic lens, the degree of conventionalization that inheres in even the clearest, most accurate photograph, is something of a shock. For, in truth, even the clearest photograph is a convention; a translation of a color transmuted into shades of black and white. In the instance to which I refer, a Bush Negro woman turned a photograph of her own son this way and that, in attempting to make sense out of the shadings of greys on the piece of paper she held. It was only when the details of the photograph were pointed out to her that she was able to perceive the subject.[16]

Starting from isolated, anecdotal experiences such as these, social psychologists began testing the influence of experience on perception in controlled environments. To select but one example, Hans H. Toch and Richard Schulte reported in 1969 on an experiment conducted at Michigan State University in which nine pairs of slides were presented to a selected group of students through an enclosed stereoscope. Each pair consisted of one "violent" and one "neutral" scene—the subject matter of the former scenes including acts of murder, theft, and suicide, that of the latter, scenes of a farmer at work, a radio announcer, and a mailman. At the exposure time of half a second, the students perceived only one of the simultaneously presented scenes (since image in the other monocular field was dominated by the one unconsciously "selected") and were asked to identify the scene observed. The groups of students consisted of sixteen advanced students in police administration, sixteen first-year students in police administration, and twenty-seven introductory psychology students. The series of slides was presented twice, in alternate eye order, so that each eye of each student was exposed to all eighteen pictures. The results showed the average number of "violent" percepts to be 9.37 for the advanced police students, 4.69 for the first-year police students, and 4.03 for the psychology students. The lowest number of violent scenes perceived by the first group was six, the highest fifteen, while for the other two groups the figures were two and nine for first-year police students and one and seven for the psychology students.

To be sure, this experiment leaves much to be desired. One might wish to have test results on the first-year police students after further training, for example, to see if there was an increase in the number of "violent" scenes perceived. But in any case, the resulting hypothesis of Toch and Schulte does not seem unwarranted. Law enforcement training, they conclude, establishes in its subjects an increased familiarity with violent scenes. Thus, "the law enforcer may come to accept crime as a familiar personal experience, one which he himself is not surprised to encounter. The acceptance of crime as a familiar experience in turn increases the ability or readiness to perceive violence where clues to it are potentially available."[17] In more general words—to a certain extent perception appears to be controlled by learning experiences.

Two years after the Toch-Schulte study, R. L. Gregory and J. G. Wallace published a monograph reporting their findings on experiments conducted with a man in his mid-fifties who, blind from very early childhood, had just recovered his sight as a result of successful corneal grafts to both eyes. They began their examination forty-eight hours after the completion of the first operation. Among the many tests administered to the subject shortly after recovery of his vision were a series of common visual illusions, "about which," Gregory and Wallace write, "a great deal is known for normal observers, even though explanations for many of them are lacking."[18] Gregory and Wallace sought the subject's responses to the Hering illusion (a parallel line distortion), the Zölner illusion (a parallel line distortion), the Poggendorf illusion (distorted continuity of a broken line), the Necker Cube (depth illusion), the Staircase Illusion (depth illusion), the Müller-Lyer illusion (length estimate illusion), and a perspective size illusion. [See Figures 1-6.] Despite good visual acuity at the time these tests were administered, the subject repeatedly failed to be "deceived" by the illusions. He had not yet *learned* to be deceived.

More recently still, anthropologist Roy G. D'Andrade administered the Kohs Block Test to a group of Hausa children in Northern Nigeria. The Kohs test, in which children are asked to arrange a group of multicolored blocks according to various drawings of identical blocks arranged in patterns, is part of a well-known I.Q. battery and has been widely praised because its nonverbal approach is supposedly culture-free. Previous investigators had found Hausa children to be very poor performers on this test and generally regarded the children's failure as evidence of poor analytic skills.

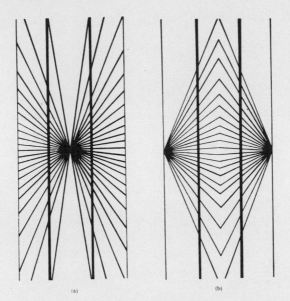

Figure 1. The Hering illusion. (a) First form. (b) Second form.

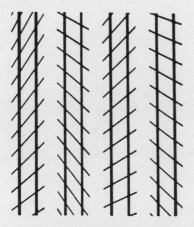

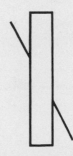

Figure 2. The Zölner illusion.   Figure 3. The Poggendorf illusion.

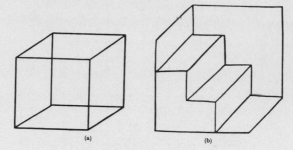

Figure 4. Ambiguous depth illusions. (a) Necker Cube. (b) Staircase illusion.

Figure 5. Müller-Lyer illusion.

Figure 6. Perspective size illusion.

130

D'Andrade discovered that the Hausa did indeed have great difficulty in copying the arrangements depicted, and further found that no matter how he adjusted the test, there was very little change in results. Finding himself at an impasse, he tried having the children copy the pattern of another *actual set of blocks* rather than the more convenient pre-drawn pictorial representations. The children's performance ratings jumped dramatically. D'Andrade then replicated this sequence successfully with a subsequent group of children from the Accra area of Ghana. Upon further investigation D'Andrade determined that *representational* pictorial or graphic art is almost totally foreign to most West African cultures, and he suggested the following explanation for the discrepancy in test scores derived from the different methods of examination:

> [West African] individuals are not only unaccustomed to the highly developed conventions of European art, such as the use of perspective, but more basically they appear to be unaccustomed to the use of line and color on flat surfaces as a means of *representation*. Designs appear to be created and appreciated not as symbols of something else, but as things in themselves. Thus it seems most probable that it is not a deficit in intelligence which makes for poor performance on the Kohs block test, but instead a lack of experience with one special method by which reality can be symbolized. The use of lines and colors on paper are such a common technique for the construction of reality for Europeans that they often believe pictures, maps, and graphs are a universal language, immediately understandable in any culture. When this turns out to be false, the first reaction seems to be to downgrade the intelligence of those who are unfamiliar with graphic representation rather than to become aware of the fact that pictures are a special way of constructing reality.[19]

It would not be difficult to fill pages with similar examples of recent studies testifying to the influence of learning or motivation on perception.[20] Instances of this phenomenon, described by John R. Platt as "the transactional relation of an organism to its environment," clearly "illustrate the idea that everything we meet—or more objectively, everything a decision-network meets—whether a human being, a stray cat, a flower, or a rock, is the other side of a feedback loop of our learning and storage system, is in some sense our cousin under creation." Thus, "the perception of an object by an organism or by this kind of decision-system involves dynamic participation by the organism. . . . To apply Martin Buber's language to this kind of objective situation, the organism cannot detect an 'it' but only an 'I-it.'"[21] Or, as Stephen C. Pepper has argued, there are "two essential elements in the perceptual act—a dynamic act of anticipatory references and a pattern of sensory materials stimulated by an environmental object as their source." As a result of this dualism, although at any given moment a multitude of light rays may be impinging on the retinas of a man's eyes, "only those which have a relevancy to his interest . . . [or, one might add, his experience-molded anticipation potential] yield perceptual material."[22] In plain language this can be seen in the everyday phenomenon of someone sleeping or reading or otherwise functioning without disturbance despite the presence of certain noises to which he or she is accustomed, but then responding alertly to another noise that, though not "objectively" different from the rest, has specific significance to that individual. This dynamic screening principle also helps account for the reverse phenomenon of finding imagined patterns of meaning in sensory materials that otherwise appear to be randomly formed: the children's game of perceiving animal shapes in clouds is one simple example; a better one, discussed earlier, is the spurious "discovery" by some of Freud's followers of the image of a vulture in Leonardo's *Anna Metterza*. In these, as in all such cases, the unique perception of significance has attained the *quality* of significance for that individual only through a process of learning, experience, or expectation.

To return to Toch and Schulte's psychology students: they had simply not *learned* to *see* in the same way as the police administration students, and they therefore saw different images of the same objective phenomena. Gregory and Wallace's newly sighted subject did not yet have enough visual knowledge of his environment to be able to be deceived by optical illusions in the same way as "normal" observers. And in the case of D'Andrade's West African children, they were unfamiliar with a form of abstract representation that most Westerners have come to regard as reflecting reality and so were unable to recognize that a two-dimensional picture was the "same thing" as the three-dimensional patterns they were creating. To sum up in psychological shorthand, there is no such thing as "immaculate perception."

Abstract and at first glance seemingly removed from the problems of psychohistory, the implications of these experiments for the psychohistorian are in fact acute. For if an individual in the past did not even *perceive* a person, event, or other seemingly "objective" phenomenon in the same way as does the modern historian, it would clearly be a mistake to apply retrospectively contemporary psychoanalytic or any other highly structured explanatory concepts of motivation to the historical figure's behavior.

But thus far we have only seen how environment and experience can affect *individual* perception. If we are to avoid the trap of solipsism and make methodologically creative use of this material, we must be able to expand the data to *some* levels of generalization. There must be shown to exist intra-cultural regularities, such as those suggested by D'Andrade—that is, some viable bases for certain generalizations (or covering laws) *within* cultures—however narrowly conceived the initial evidence for such generalizations may be.[23] The first large-scale work on this problem was begun two decades ago by a team of psychologists and anthropologists at Northwestern University.

In the Preface to their study, *The Influence of Culture on Visual Perception,* Marshall H. Segall and Donald T. Campbell offered the background rationale for initiating their work:

> A running debate at Northwestern University between Melville Herskovits and Donald Campbell, in which the former stressed that cultural differences might well be of sufficient magnitude to influence perceptual tendencies and the latter argued that the biological homogeneity of culture-learning man would preclude such influence, led to the decision, in 1956, to go into the field with the appropriate psychological instruments and techniques and attack the problem empirically.[24]

The result of their study was an extensive report, covering their own research and the historical background of the subject. Of principal concern to us, however, is what Segall, Campbell, and Herskovits called their "carpentered-world hypothesis":

> Western societies provide environments replete with rectangular objects; these objects, when projected on the retina, are represented by nonrectangular images. For the people living in carpentered worlds, the tendency to interpret obtuse and acute angles in retinal images as deriving from rectangular objects is likely to be so pervasively reinforced that it becomes automatic and unconscious relatively early in life. For those living where man-made structures are a small portion of the visual environment and where such structures are constructed without benefit of carpenters' tools (saw, plane, straight edge, tape measure, carpenter's square, spirit level, plumb bob, chalk line, surveyor's sight, etc.), straight lines and precise right angles are a rarity. As a result, the inference habit of interpreting acute and obtuse angles as right angles extended in space would not be learned, at least not as well.[25]

Since, in general, "European and American city dwellers have a much higher percentage of rectangularity in their environments than any residents of non-Europeanized cultures," Segall, Campbell, and Herskovits predicted "that people who live in non-Western environments would be *less* susceptible than Western peoples to the illusions typically noted with these figures [the Sander parallelogram and Müller-Lyer diagrams and a perspective drawing illusion]."[26] [See Figures 5, 7 and 8.] The tendency of people living in "carpentered" environments to interpret two-dimensional forms as representations of three-dimensional objects should, they reasoned, make them particularly susceptible to such illusions. On the other hand, since horizontal-vertical illusions would then have "more ecological validity for peoples living mostly outdoors in open, spacious environments, it is predicted that such peoples will be more susceptible than Western peoples in urban environments" to *that* sort of illusion.[27]

The research team established seventeen different cultural groups for testing, from residents of the Ankole District of Uganda to those of Evanston, Illinois—a total of nearly 2,000 respondents. Each respondent was tested for his or her reactions to fifty drawings representing five basic geometric illusions. Extensive, careful analysis of the procedures and received data take up well over one hundred pages in the published report, but in short, the considerable support found for both of the hypotheses described above led the authors to conclude:

> Perception is an aspect of human behavior, and as such it is subject to many of the same influences that shape other aspects of behavior. In particular, each individual's experiences combine in a complex fashion to determine his reaction to a given stimulus situation. *To the extent that certain classes of experiences are more likely to occur in some cultures than in others, differences in behavior across cultures, including differences in perceptual ten-*

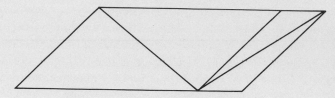

Figure 7. The Sander parallelogram illusion

Figure 8. The perspective drawing illusion

dencies, can be great enough even to surpass the ever-present individual differences within cultural groupings. . . . The findings we have reported, and the findings of others we have reviewed, point to the conclusion that to a substantial extent *we learn to perceive;* that in spite of the phenomenally absolute character of our perceptions, they are determined by perceptual inference habits; and that *various inference habits are differentially likely in differ-*

ent societies. For all mankind, the basic process of perception is the same; only the contents differ and these differ only because they reflect different perceptual inference habits.[28]

The significance for the historian of the foregoing quotation should be fairly readily apparent. In terms of visual perception, a keystone of motivation and action, people are not "the same" in all places at all times. The structure of their environments and the values and standards of the cultures and subcultures of which they are a part have a powerfully coercive influence on the apparent nature of the very objects that they see. As George S. Klein has put it, "perception is an adaptive cognitive act, *always* rooted in the intentional life of the person, in his motives and aims vis-à-vis the environment."[29] Further, studies and conclusions similar to those cited above formed much of the basis for Thomas S. Kuhn's chapter on world-view in his now almost classic study, *The Structure of Scientific Revolutions:* "Surveying the rich experimental literature from which these examples are drawn," he writes, "makes one suspect that something like a paradigm [the shared assumptions of a given community] is prerequisite to perception itself."[30] As paradigms change, then so must perception.

Thus far, this argument has emphasized the one-directional effects of environmental and cultural learning on perception. Critical to an understanding of the importance of these effects is the reverse of this phenomenon: the effect of perception on learning and motivation. Because of its seeming obviousness,[31] the effect of perception on learning and motivation has received little recent study.[32] As George Klein has pointed out, however: "in a context of action, perception is both a condition for changing behavior (a 'stimulus') and a response. We act *in terms of* the meaning and quality of a percept. It is tied up with intention and with consequences in action, producing a change in one's relations in the environment."[33] The effects of this interactional influence between perception and action, while endlessly individuated on one level, are not necessarily always so random. Not only is this superficially obvious—people within specified cultural contexts do perceive objects, symbols, and other people in at least *functionally* similar ways (otherwise communication would be impossible)—but it is empirically verified in the evidence of intracultural regularity found in the work of D'Andrade and of Segall, Campbell, and Herskovits, and others. The objection of solipsism, in other words, is not tenable in this case any more than it is in the mind-body controversy discussed in a previous chapter.[34]

* * *

The work just discussed has been concerned only with object perception. Studies of this sort are easiest to design, analyze, and replicate with a body of well-anchored controls, and they are of primary importance because they show beyond doubt that perception is a dynamic process that mutually *influences and is influenced by* the perceiver's environment, knowledge, and attitudes. Further, these studies indicate that although the quality of a percept can in theory be unique to a single individual, in fact there are most often broad *similarities* in terms of object perception *within* cultures and social groups at the same time that there are often great *dis*similarities *among different* cultures and social groups.

It must be acknowledged here that, in order to conduct this sort of analysis with requisite scientific care and rigor, the specific questions asked have of course had to be drastically narrowed from those posed by Levy-Bruhl and others early in this century. Thus, grand conjectures as to whether or not pre-industrial peoples "think" like us have been translated into studies of whether or not people in different cultures respond similarly to optical illusions, or whether or not children in different environments will make similar judgments

regarding quantity when substances are presented in differently
shaped containers. Slowly but surely the questions being asked are
growing in complexity and overall significance. But even at present
these studies in psychological anthropology have shown, and continue to show, that in the most fundamentally cognitive ways people
in different cultures often do dramatically differ from one another.
The revolutionary importance of this for students of human behavior should not be overlooked: despite all the questions that remain
to be explored we now have clear scientific support for the idea that
in the conduct of research on human subjects culturally removed
from us we can no longer assume what the social philosopher Alfred
Schutz termed a "reciprocity of perspectives" regarding the researcher's and the researcher's subjects' basic views of the world.[35]
On the other hand, and of equal importance, because certain intra-
cultural generalizations can be made, we are not necessarily trapped
by a self-defeating radical scepticism about any knowledge of others.

In viewing the world, however, people perceive more than inanimate objects. They also perceive other people and other people's
apparent emotions and attitudes—and they perceive the various
forces and unstructured elements in the world and universe about
themselves, *giving* structure to those elements and responding *to*
that created structure in the process. Thus, objects of perception are
social and cosmological as well as physical. They include concepts
of time and space, order and disorder, truth and falsehood, good and
evil, practicality and impracticality, pleasure and displeasure, cause
and effect, autonomy and dependence, harmony and conflict, justice
and injustice, reality and unreality (and, of course, confinement and
freedom, cleanliness and uncleanliness)—to name but a few of the
countless cognitive assumptions, simultaneously derived from and
created by perception, that people in all times and places have
always brought with them to the unexamined, down-to-earth hum-
drum of everyday life.

Despite individual variances, and without arguing for a naïve *tab-*

ula rasa model of human growth, it is clear that people are born into and cognitively formed by very general belief systems in the same way that they are born into and formed by language systems. As Clifford Geertz has observed: "Just as no man has to invent a language in order to speak, so no man has to invent a religion in order to worship."[36] It could readily be added that one does not have to invent a time framework, an ethical system, or a life-cycle model in order to effectively function as a social being. On the contrary, a framework for effective functioning is provided by the cultural definitions of reality each individual inherits and absorbs as he or she moves into and through life in a particular cultural milieu. But, it is the conclusion of a wealth of studies throughout several decades of research in anthropology and cross-cultural psychology that—as with object perceptions—cognitive assumptions of this sort vary dramatically from culture to culture.[37]

Probably the most striking and well-known example of this sort of phenomenon was provided by Walter B. Cannon almost thirty years ago when he published his pioneering and now classic essay, "'Voodoo' Death."[38] In that work, which Claude Lévi-Strauss was to use as the initial insight in his later arguments concerning the cognitive power of magic and religion,[39] Cannon showed how physiological responses up to and including death could result from "a particularly intense activity of the sympathetic nervous system" in response to the *perceived* reality of spiritual threat within a specified cultural context that defines such threats as *real*. Other examples of the sharp cognitive differences that are found among cultures range from the seemingly impossible open-sea navigational skills of Trukese canoeists, to the elaborate taxonomies known among indigenous Philippine and American peoples of seemingly (to others) indistinct plant, reptile, and weather categories; from the extreme respect for individual autonomy from earliest infancy among the Sikhs in British Columbia and the Wintu of California, to the very great insistence upon interdependence and collectivity among the

Wolof of Senegal; from the constricted time frame of certain Melanesian and African peoples, to the linear "envelope" of time of Judaic-Christian tradition; from the phenomenon of *machismo* in certain Latin cultures, to that of paralyzing social "stage fright" in Bali; from the idea among the Navaho that certain kinds of insanity are caused by moths in one's head, to the idea among some European-Americans that certain kinds of insanity are the result of a battle among a trinity of mystical forces in the mind that are called *id, ego,* and *superego*.[40]

A list of this sort could, of course, go on and on. To find fascination in differences of this nature is a common pastime among undergraduate students of anthropology. But it is *not* commonly recognized that similar lists can be drawn up regarding peoples separated from us by *time* rather than by space. Temporal distance, I am suggesting, can be at least as profoundly influential in this regard as spatial distance; that is, the subjects of historical inquiry differ from those of anthropological inquiry only in the specific *manner* of their differentness and in the relative scantiness and obscurity of evidence to study. While we will probably never know (nor may we care) how uniquely a thirteenth-century burgher, a medieval Samurai, or a seventeenth-century Quaker housewife would have interpreted the Müller-Lyer illusion, we can know and should care about the vast differences in *general* perceptual and cognitive assumptions prevailing in the various worlds of the past. And the best of historians have recognized this for a very long time.

A sense of that differentness infuses the pages of Huizinga's great work, *The Waning of the Middle Ages.* It is dealt with directly in Ariès's complex studies of childhood, family, and death. The world of perception has been treated with insight by D. W. Robertson, William J. Brandt, and, with special sensitivity, Carolly Erickson. Dramatic shifts in the Western sense of space depth and shape have been described by Thomas Kuhn and Alexandre Koyré. The richness of differences in material life has been discussed at length by Braudel.

The gulf separating early medieval and later concepts of individuality and collectivity has been examined by Colin Morris. Radically different concepts of time and the shape of history in Western thought have been studied by Peter Burke. Abrupt and deep shifts in modes of discourse concerning madness, criminality, sickness, sex, and other subjects have been analyzed by Foucault. The deep importance of magic in history has been discussed by Keith Thomas. Dramatic changes in sexual and marital patterns have been demonstrated by Lawrence Stone. A brief but important view of infanticide in history has been given us by Maria W. Piers. The impact of evolving "manners" and long-term changes in personal affect and control structures has been described by Norbert Elias.[41] These are only a few recent examples from the study of European history since the Middle Ages, but the certain implication in the substance of all this work is that, in the words of the Dutch psychoanalyst J. H. van den Berg, "earlier generations lived a different sort of life . . . [and] were *essentially* different from us.[42]

For some reason—probably because the act of writing history provides and imposes upon its data a false sense of identifiable, unfolding tradition, whereas anthropology involves abrupt discovery and the shock of anachronism—historians have yet to fully confront the revolutionary importance of much of the work they have themselves done during the past few decades. It was not so very long ago that a similar state of affairs existed in anthropology. But the compelling quality of fundamental human difference among so-called primitive peoples that was the anthropologist's stock-in-trade—and the further perceived differences between those peoples and themselves— could not long be ignored. Doubtless this also accounts for the fact that the earliest and most complete discussions to date among historians of such essential differences are to be found among medievalists. Just as anthropology, however, rapidly moved from analysis of the most distant and seemingly bizarre cultural settings to others closer to home, so are historians now beginning to see that they need not look so far back in time as the Middle Ages to find evidence of dramatic cognitive differences between themselves and their historical subjects.

It thus seems clear that even if psychoanalytic theory were an effective technique for understanding the world of the present, it would be a hopeless exercise in intellectual myopia to apply it to the past. As is true with anthropologists—who have the dual benefits of a head start in research of this sort and the luxury of communities of living subjects to question—historians have before them the task of more carefully structuring their conceptual arguments, in a sense, from the inside out to conform with the recognition that they do not share a reciprocity of cognitive perspectives with their subjects.[43] Nevertheless, at the very least, the substantive richness of the best recent work in history inevitably supports the minimal conclusion that any elaborate culture-bound theory of behavioral explanation (even one, unlike psychoanalysis, of logical soundness and empirical validity) is destined to a large measure of failure in attempting to analyze the various worlds of the past.

What is ironic about this fact is that, while numerous historians (who, of all people, should be sensitive to such matters) have of late been indiscriminately ripping their subjects of inquiry out of historical context and analyzing them through the borrowed lenses of psychoanalytic hypothesis, a number of prominent psychoanalysts have themselves spoken out on the necessary failure of such an enterprise.

Over twenty years ago Heinz Kohut (at present a fashionable figure among the more avant-garde psychohistorians) warned his colleagues of the dangers inherent in psychoanalytic explanations that failed to first, through introspection and empathy, take careful account of the problem of anachronism. Of course, Kohut assumed that once this imaginative leap was performed (an operation not unlike that advocated by R. G. Collingwood two decades earlier) psychoanalysis was still a viable tool. More recently, however, Edgar A. Levenson, Director of Clinical Services and Training and Supervising Analyst at the William Alanson White Institute of Psychiatry, Psychoanalysis, and Psychology, went still further. In an expansion of remarks made to a twenty-fifth anniversary gathering of Institute Fellows, he argued that the failure of his colleagues to recognize "the ephemeral time-bound nature" of the psychoanalytic enterprise was responsible for the great "disarray in the theory and practice of psychoanalysis" that currently exists—not the least of which involves the "entirely gratuitous operation" of "reanalyzing the patients of the past." Then, drawing explicitly on the historical work of Thomas Kuhn, Phillippe Ariès, and others, he pointed to the "pervasive nonsense" of those (Erikson is mentioned specifically) who insist on applying contemporary psychoanalytic models to noncontemporary subjects. With particular reference to Ariès' findings concerning the conventionality of adult-child sexual play in certain cultures Levenson went on: "The assumption that a sexually diddled Moslem boy, a Japanese child sharing his parents' sleeping quarters or a Victorian fourteen-year-old girl being seduced by a mature man [a reference to Freud's famous "Dora"] would all have reactions we, in our era, can predict or empathize with is an egregious error, a magnificent arrogance of time and place." Put simply, in less flamboyant language: "a contemporary psychoanalyst attempting to extrapolate his own experience to another period would be in error."[44] Would that historians might learn from this leading psychoanalyst what he has learned from them.

6

"If often he was wrong and at times absurd,
To us he is no more a person
Now but a whole climate of opinion . . . "

—W. H. Auden,
"In Memory of
Sigmund Freud"

The Failure
of Psychohistory

IT is time now to do some stock taking and to consider the general consequences (and some possible objections to them) of what we have observed in the preceding pages.

We have seen that, from the earliest endeavors to write psychohistory to those of the present, individual writings of would-be psychohistorians have consistently been characterized by a cavalier attitude toward fact, a contorted attitude toward logic, an irresponsible attitude toward theory validation, and a myopic attitude toward cultural difference and anachronism. Some will object that, though this may be so, psychohistory is still a youthful genre and one cannot satisfactorily dismiss a *method* of analysis merely by pointing out flaws in the work of individual practitioners. Although repeated failures of this sort should at least suggest cause for reflection, we have accepted this objection as having a certain validity. Thus, we proceeded to examine psychoanalytic theory itself—the theoretical underpinning of psychohistory—to see how well it dealt with these same problems.

We have seen that psychoanalysis is unable to provide acceptable evidence to indicate that it is more successful as a therapeutic device than any other form of recognized therapy. Further, it is an open question whether psychoanalysis is even any more therapeutically successful than simple informal palliative techniques of providing general comfort and personal encouragement. It may be objected that this is not in itself a sufficient measure of theoretical validity, since there are phenomena in other fields (medicine for one, economics for another) that can be rather well explained by theory, but that cannot—at least yet—be much altered or manipulated by formal intervention. This is true. However, when there are a *variety* of competing explanatory theories in force, all of which are equally successful (or unsuccessful) in effecting change in the phenomena in question, at the very least we have no grounds for accepting the explanatory scheme of any one over the others. To the extent, then, that therapeutic efficacy is a valid criterion for evaluating the truth claims of a generically therapeutic technique that subsequently evolved into a system designed to explain human thought and behavior—and, if not sufficient unto itself, such a criterion is certainly not wholly irrelevant—it must be concluded that psychoanalytic theory holds no place of positive distinction among its competitors, many of which take directly contradictory theoretical stances. If, nevertheless, we are willing to admit that lack of therapeutic distinction is of itself insufficient ground for dismissing psychoanalytic theory, we are led to press matters further: to examine the logical structure of that theory.

We have seen that psychoanalytic theory is riddled with crippling logical inadequacies. Among the fallacies discussed—any one of which may be sufficient to cause the logical collapse of the system— was its willful effort to resist disconfirmation by claiming that *any* eventuality is covered and can be explained by the presence or absence of the so-called defense mechanisms of reaction-formation, displacement, sublimation, and the like. Although this apparent ability to explain everything has no doubt contributed to the popular appeal of psychoanalysis (as it has with astrology), it flatly disqualifies psychoanalytic theory from any consideration as a theory of scientific or even logically respectable explanation. Still, it can be argued, it is not impossible that psychoanalytic theory may lead to the occasional discovery of a psychological fact. Just as there is anecdotal evidence of therapeutic efficacy (as there is for all therapies) which is totally independent of theory invalidation, so too can there be anecdotal support for phenomena identification which is totally independent of logical failure. This is true, as it is for theories of character explanation based on physiognomy, climate, race, sex, physique, or any of a large number of things, including the date and time of one's birth. For example, it is *possible* that an apparently significant number of people who are weaned early, or who have large noses, or who live in the tropics—and so on—may *appear* to be characterologically marked in some way. It is also true that an observation of such apparent fact may derive from the application of a theory that is blatantly nonsensical. While it is essential to recognize that such an observation would not save the *theory* from rejection, it does deserve some attention and testing—first to see if the claimed discovery is true, and second (if it does appear to be true) to see if it is true because of the claimed causal sequence.[1] Assuming for the sake of argument that early-weaned individuals can be shown to manifest certain character traits, can it be shown that early weaning is the *cause* of these traits, as hypothesized, rather than merely another *symptom* of something else (in this case, perhaps, a generally rejecting maternal attitude)? This was the subject we explored next.

We have seen that the psychological facts allegedly discovered as a result of the employment of psychoanalytic theory are drastically few in number and even then are not beyond serious dispute; for the most part they are trivial; and further, no good evidence exists to establish the validity of psychoanalytically posited causality. To take one example that was discussed, there is some indication (though it remains challenged by many experimental psychologists) that the character traits of frugality, obstinacy, and orderliness tend to cluster in individual personalities. Without evidence to support the psychoanalyst's contention that these traits derive from childhood experience, however, this observation is of negligible psychological value—and no such evidence exists. Indeed, quite apart from the matter of specific psychoanalytic hypotheses, the best modern research now firmly indicates that there are *no* psychological structures established in early childhood that are sufficiently resilient to survive into adulthood without constant environmental support. Moreover, this quality of psychological malleability clearly remains present *after* adulthood is attained.[2] The objections of the analyst to all this are predictable: the theory is so subtle and complex, it is said, that we are not sufficiently advanced in science to adequately test it; or, we have misunderstood the psychoanalytic method, it is claimed: what matters to the individual is not what happened in early childhood, but what, lost in his or her unconscious, the individual unknowingly *thinks* happened—an approach that not only moves psychoanalytic theory to the realm of the mystical, but that also makes methodologically impossible its transfer to the analysis of historical data. In any case, it is this sort of response, added to everything else reviewed here, that has led many of the normally most even-tempered of scientists to conclude, with P. B. Medawar, that "psychoanalytic theory is the most stupendous intellectual confidence trick of the twentieth century and a terminal product as well—something akin to a dinosaur or zeppelin in the history of ideas, a vast structure of radically unsound design and with no posterity."[3]

Psychoanalytic theory may well be that. It probably is that. But even if we were to *accept* the psychoanalyst's dissembling explanations for the failure to scientifically confirm psychoanaytic theory, what would we be left with? We would be left with a fanciful collection of patently illogical and as yet unverified notions that are not even especially effective when put to their primary use, which is therapy. That any historian would use this sort of thing as a system to guide him in explaining the past seems incredible. Still, in the preceding pages we took matters yet one step further and found that even if psychoanalytic theory were logical, confirmed, and therapeutically effective in the present there is little chance that it would be a useful explanatory tool when applied to the past.

Psychohistory, in a word, is ahistorical. That is its ultimate failing. Perhaps the single most important achievement of modern historical thinking has been the growing recognition on the part of the historian that life in the past was marked by a fundamental social and cognitive differentness from that prevailing in our own time. Although the detailed exploration of those differences (concepts of time, space, causation, reality, personhood, sexuality, and the like) has only very recently begun, the *recognition* of such differences is an accomplishment comparable to the similar revolution in anthropology of half a century ago. It is, therefore, particularly ironical that the fashion of explaining the past by simplistically applying to it an illogical and ineffective collection of narcissistically contemporary notions should reach such heights just when the best work of an important generation of historians has begun to show how sadly anachronistic *any* such present-biased explanation system must be. Indeed, it is an irony of especial pungency when it is recognized that the labors of one particularly zealous group of psychohistorians— those associated with the *Journal of Psychohistory*—have resulted in a small mountain of data that undermines their own interests. In their missionary determination to find evidence that "the history of childhood is a nightmare from which we have just begun to awaken," these writers have unearthed a substantial body of material on subjects ranging from infanticide to child rearing that is itself (even considering their frequent distortions and exaggerations) striking testimony to the discontinous nature of historical experience and the utter irrelevance of modern psychoanalysis in attempting to understand that experience.

*   *   *

The ideas of psychoanalysis have become, as Lionel Trilling once remarked, "the slang of our culture."[4] While this doubtless helps account for the uncritical public acceptance of much recent psychohistory, it should also serve to suggest to us something else: slang, after all, is that most ephemeral and transitory of vocabularies. History is a very old discipline. It has endured much, including ever waxing and waning exhortations to embark on "new approaches," "scientific analyses," and "next assignments." To subsequent generations such endeavors as often as not appear ludicrous—as eventually, no doubt, will most of the artifacts of the current vogue of history-as-applied-psychoanalysis. But *as artifacts* those writings will not be without interest, for they will someday be testimony to a time when people attempted once more to codify aspects of what had become the commonsense realities of their brief historical instant and to use that codification to explain not only their lives but those of all others who had gone before them.

It should not be asking too much to suggest that historians might have a sense of history. Every historical epoch has its own rarely examined, taken-for-granted climate of opinion on matters pertaining to the past as well as the present. We live in a time perhaps more intellectually restless than most, and those who are restless sometimes seek quietude in one form or another of historical determinism—as they always have.

The seventeenth century was another time of intellectual restlessness. In that it was an era of enormous scientific achievement and tumultuous social upheaval, it was an era not entirely incomparable to our own. It was also an era that found the lure of historical determinism irresistible, though of course it was a form of determinism appropriate to the moment. Just as the modern psychohistorian may turn to Grinstein's *Psychoanalytic Index* for the ever-available keys to unlock the mysteries of his or her craft, so the writer of the seventeenth century turned to his own guidebook to the past and the present. He called it Scripture, and it, too, answered every question. The universe, to the historian of the seventeenth century, was in an ongoing state of decay, spiraling ever downward from an original divinely created state of perfection. With this sense of revealed truth firmly in mind, there was no human question that lay beyond the realm of answer. Indeed, so firmly rooted in its own cultural element was this infallible and irrefutable explanation system, that those who attempted to dislodge it encountered the same sort of imbedded dogmatism as have those who in recent years have raised questions about psychohistory and the psychoanalytic climate of opinion. Thus, George Hakewill wrote in 1627, "the opinion of the world's decay is so generally received, not only among the vulgar, but of the learned, both divines and others, that the very commonness of it makes it current with many, without any further examination."[5]

But, of course, even "the very commonness" of that universal explanatory scheme gave way in time to the demand for evidence— evidence exogenous to its own hermetically sealed and endlessly self-proving logical framework. Despite its own successful insinuation into the popular discourse of our time (as C. P. Snow once observed, "a prediliction for Freudian analysis has become as much an American preserve as high-school basketball or Thanksgiving dinner") psychoanalytic theory has now begun to succumb to the same fate.[6]

For some time psychoanalytic theory has been under attack from what has appeared to be opposite directions: some have found fault with what they regard as its repellant "mechanization" of mind, while others have stressed its scientific nonvalidity. In fact, these are not uncomplementary accusations: it is, as we have seen, *both* unrealistically mechanistic *and* helplessly unscientific. There should thus be little cause for wonder when it is pointed out that, among its varied progeny, the stripling calling itself "psychohistory" has little chance for survival.

It could not be otherwise. For, like the religion-based idea of the world's decay, psychoanalytic theory, in any and all of its guises, is an illusion—ironically enough, in the Freudian sense of that word. An illusion, observed Freud, is not necessarily *always* in contradiction to reality (thus it is different from a delusion, though often bordering on it), but is most clearly marked by an element of wish-fulfillment. Though "insusceptible of proof," Freud wrote, and often "so improbable, so incompatible with everything we have laboriously discovered about the reality of the world, that we may compare them—if we pay proper regard to the psychological differences—to delusions," illusions are clung to by many because they provide ready answers to an entire range of otherwise unbearably unanswerable questions. Indeed, Freud observed, "in other matters no sensible person will behave so irresponsibly or rest content with such feeble grounds for his opinions" as one does when one is faced with matters of such great personal importance, matters in which one has invested so much. Freud was, of course, here speaking of religion. The same sort of resistance, however, in the name of which "people are guilty of every possible sort of dishonesty and intellectual misdemeanor," is now encountered everywhere in the wish-fulfilling writings of the embattled defenders of psychoanalytic theory and psychohistory.[7]

It is part of the very nature of scholarly endeavor, in the humanities as well as the sciences, to evolve new understanding of phenomena by maintaining a vibrant tension between the processes of hypothesis and critique. On occasion, however, hypothesizing can become so shoddy, extravagant, and woolly-minded that the essential tension between creativity and responsibility is broken—and the possibility of genuine new understanding disappears. What emerges instead, floating free of the restraints of logical and empirical rigor, are quirky, dogmatic, often oracular, and wholly unverified—indeed, illusory—pronouncements. In the sciences, prominent and relatively recent examples of such pronouncements range from Immanuel Velikovsky's attempted validation of the mythologically-described events of various cultures by imagining the existence of certain catastrophes in the solar system to Erich von Däniken's effort to explain certain archeological puzzles by relying on the fantasied existence of a race of ancient astronauts.[8] In the humanities the best recent examples of such excess belong to the world of psychohistory.

Perhaps, however, future historians will see in psychohistory's small legacy something of value—something in content certainly of less historical significance, but in form not unlike the legacy of the pseudosciences of the nineteenth century. Phrenology, animal magnetism, Mesmerism and the like may have properly seemed "coarse and odious to scientific men," Ralph Waldo Emerson once observed, but there was at least associated with them and their times "a breath of new air, much vague expectation, a consciousness of power not yet finding its determinate aim."[9] Among psychohistorians, only Erik Erikson has produced work that, despite its evident limitations, might be deserving of such praise—and Erikson, not coincidentally, has of late publically tried to disassociate his work from that of other practitioners of the craft.[10] Still, for all its manifold failings (to say nothing of its "coarseness and odiousness"), psychohistory has somewhat jarred the profession of history. It has forced that profession to look a bit more carefully at its standards and purposes, and it has insisted that deeper analyses of traditional historical data are both possible and necessary. While it is now obvious that such analyses cannot successfully be conducted by psychoanalytic techniques, by forcing an array of unorthodox modes of inquiry into the ongoing text of historical discourse the psychohistorian may have helped facilitate an awakening of sorts in the historical imagination—an awakening marked by a willingness to ask different questions.

It has been most common among historians in general to resist psychohistorical explanation by vaguely and tentatively asserting that the specific behavioral explanatory models of one era cannot appropriately be transferred to another. All the available evidence now indicates that, at the very least, there is no need for timidity in making this claim. But perhaps the very challenge of psychoanalytic explanation will in time be seen to have inspired, admittedly by way of protest, a general sensitivity among historians to the need for building temporally bound explanation schemes from the inside out—that is, for initiating analysis from within the cultural confines of the common sense world being studied, rather than imposing on that world highly structured, abstract, empirically unverified, present-biased systems that are inherently distorting.

It must now be stated plainly, however, that if this much can be said for the value of psychohistory, it is all that can be said. Traditional criticisms concerning vulgarity, reductionism, trivialization, and the like all remain valid observations on the psychohistorical enterprise. But the most important and fundamental reason for the rejection of that enterprise is now clear: psychohistory does not work and cannot work. The time has come to face the fact that, behind all its rhetorical posturing, the psychoanalytic approach to history is—irremediably—one of logical perversity, scientific unsoundness, and cultural naïveté. The time has come, in short, to move on.

Notes

Preface

1. Claude Lévi-Strauss, *Structural Anthropology* [orig. pub. 1958] (New York: Basic Books, 1963), pp. 18–19.

2. William L. Langer, "The Next Assignment," *American Historical Review*, 63 (1958): 283–304.

3. H. Stuart Hughes, *History as Art and as Science* (New York: Harper, 1964), p. 65.

4. Fawn M. Brodie, "Who Defends the Abolitionist?" in *The Antislavery Vanguard: New Essays on the Abolitionists*, ed. Martin Duberman (Princeton, N.J.: Princeton University Press, 1965), p. 66. Brodie is here referring to the work of David Donald, a man who, she says, wields "a deft scalpel" and "lays bare certain signs of impotence and latent homosexuality in his hero with such subtlety that the reader is scarcely aware that he is witnessing a surgical operation."

5. These journals—and they should not be confused—are *The Journal of Psychohistory* (formerly *The History of Childhood Quarterly*) and *The Psychohistory Review*. The latter publication is much the more serious, responsible, intelligent, and self-critical of the two.

6. Lloyd de Mause, "The Independence of Psychohistory," in de Mause, ed., *The New Psychohistory* (New York: Psychohistory Press, 1975), pp. 22-23.

7. Ibid., pp. 23-24.

8. Ibid., p. 25.

9. See, for example, John Demos's scathing review of Glenn Davis's *Childhood and History in America* (a product of de Mause's psychohistorical cottage industry), which also contains remarks on de Mause's declaration of independence: *The New York Times Book Review* (April 24, 1977), p. 11.

10. See, for instance, Jacques Barzun, *Clio and the Doctors: Psychohistory, Quanto-history, and History* (Chicago: University of Chicago Press, 1974); Gertrude Himmelfarb, "The 'New History,'" *Commentary*, 59 (January 1975); and Charles Krauthammer, "The Expanding Shrink," *The New Republic* (September 22, 1979).

11. Barzun, *Clio and the Doctors*, p. 158. This comment and the one that precedes it should not be taken as a wholesale rejection of Barzun's fine and eloquent book; on the contrary, I admire his wisdom and erudition, share most of his views, and have learned much from him—but I believe our respective works are addressed to different generations of historians.

12. Sigmund Freud, "An Autobiographical Study," in *Standard Edition of the Complete Psychological Works of Sigmund Freud*, ed. James Strachey (London: Hogarth Press, 1961), vol. 20, p. 50.

13. See, for example, David Shakow and David Rapaport's dismissal of an experimental psychologist's criticism of psychoanalysis in which they claim that the lack of confirming evidence for the psychoanalytic hypothesis "stems from the inadequacy of the available methods for studying the kind of complex relationship he is surveying." David Shakow and David Rapaport, *The Influence of Freud on American Psychology* (New York: International Universities Press, 1964), p. 177.

14. For Freud on this and on his other complaint that anti-Semitism lay behind his critics' motives, see "The Resistance to Psycho-analysis," in *Standard Edition*, ed. Strachey, vol. 19, p. 222; and "The Question of Lay Analysis," ibid., vol. 20, p. 207.

15. Erik H. Erikson, *Young Man Luther: A Study in Psychoanalysis and History* (New York: Norton, 1958), p. 8. See also, along with remarks intended to distance his work from that of other efforts in the field, Erikson's reassertion that psychohistory "is the study of individual and collective life with the combined methods of psychoanalysis and history." Erik H.

Erikson, *Dimensions of a New Identity* (New York: Norton, 1974), pp. 12–13. In addition, note that in an ongoing series of bibliographical articles attempting to explore "Alternatives to Psychoanalytic Psychohistory" (which identifies not a *single* published work self-identified as substantive psychohistory that is *not* psychoanalytically grounded) William Gilmore admits that "the majority of psychohistorians accept . . . as a sensible working definition of psychohistory" an approach guided by a psychoanalytic method that (here he quotes Bruce Mazlish) "emphasizes ego and superego as well as id factors, and that pays special attention to defensive and adaptive mechanisms." "Mainstream psychohistory," he concludes (meaning everything *but* the work of de Mause and associates as well as a vague and ill-defined something called "the history of personality") "is decidedly psychoanalytic psychohistory, however explicit or implicit the theory." *The Psychohistory Review*, 7 (1979): 44.

16. I am excluding with these remarks the work of behaviorists and experimental psychologists not because their work is not of potential interest to the historian, but simply because it has been so infrequently used. This is so even for a figure like Piaget whose developmental findings might seem of especial interest to historians. Perhaps historians have been less interested in more scientifically-based psychological theory because the theorists themselves have (unlike psychoanalysts) not been much interested in the applicability of their work to the lives of historical figures—and perhaps *this* is so because, as Robert Coles suggests, "a scientist like Piaget knows full well that the 'variables' that make up a man's creative life—be it a writer's or a political leader's or a psychoanlyst's—defy the language and concepts of any particular psychological theory." See Robert Coles, *The Mind's Fate: Ways of Seeing Psychiatry and Psychoanalysis* (Boston: Little, Brown, 1975), p. 192. The work referred to by Weinstein and Platt includes *The Wish to be Free* (Berkeley: University of California Press, 1970) and *Psychoanalytic Sociology* (Baltimore: Johns Hopkins University Press, 1973).

17. For some general remarks on this, see Freud's "Introductory Lectures on Psycho-analysis," Part III, Lecture XXVII, in *Standard Edition*, ed. Strachey, vol. 16, pp. 431–37.

18. Freud, "'Wild' Psycho-analysis," in *Standard Edition*, ed. Strachey, vol. 11, pp. 219–230. Freud expressed great concern in this paper that such superficial and uncontrolled uses of psychoanalytic ideas, without lengthy personal contact with individual patients, would do serious harm to the cause of psychoanalysis. Then, in that same year (1910), Freud published his own "wild" analysis of Leonardo da Vinci.

Chapter One

1. There are several editions of Freud's book on Leonardo. All references and citations that follow are from the *Standard Edition of the Complete Psychological Works of Sigmund Freud*, translated by Alan Tyson and published as a separate volume by W. W. Norton (New York, 1964).

2. Joseph D. Lichtenberg, "Freud's Leonardo: Psychobiography and Autobiography of Genius," *Journal of the American Psychoanalytic Association*, 26 (1978): 863.

3. The Jung discovery was not published, but it was mentioned by Freud in a letter to Pfister and is noted along with Pfister's "more convincing" and published revelation in Ernest Jones, *The Life and Work of Sigmund Freud* (New York: Basic Books, 1955), vol. II, p. 348. The Stites discovery is reported in his note, "More on Freud's Leonardo," *College Art Journal*, 8 (1948): 40. The italics in the citation from Freud are in the original.

4. Eric Maclagan, "Leonardo in the Consulting Room," *Burlington Magazine*, XLII (1923): 54-57.

5. See Jones, *Life and Work*, vol. II, p. 348; Freud, *Leonardo da Vinci* (editor's note), p. 10; K. R. Eissler, *Leonardo da Vinci: Psychoanalytic Notes on the Enigma* (New York: International Universities Press, 1961), p. 14; and Lichtenberg, "Freud's Leonardo."

6. See Emil Möller, "Der Geburtstag des Lionardo da Vinci," *Jahrbuch der preussischen Kunstsammlungen*, 60 (1939). Möller shows in this piece that Leonardo's paternal grandfather recorded his birth and baptism in the family diary and also named ten godparents, mostly neighbors of the paternal household, for the infant. At the very least this suggests that Leonardo was born in his father's home and was accepted immediately as a member of the household. This suggestion becomes more compelling when connected with the next document we have concerning Leonardo, which shows him still to be a member of his father's household at age five. Freud's contention, on the contrary, rests on no historical evidence whatsoever.

7. On the matter of castration anxiety and homosexuality the work most supportive of Freud is reported in L. Bieber et. al, *Homosexuality: A Psychoanalytic Study of Male Homosexuals* (New York: Basic Books, 1962). It must be noted, however, that the evidence used in this study was limited to clinical *impressions* of patients, not direct study, and that it lends only metaphorical support to Freud in concluding that the homosexuals observed may have felt "more physically vulnerable" when growing up than did heterosexuals—a long way from castration anxiety, and a finding that, in a

homophobic culture, may indeed be regarded as a simple and accurately perceived statement of fact. The more important recent studies have found virtually no support for Freud. See, for example, J. N. DeLuca, "Performance of Overt Male Homosexuals and Controls on the Blacky Test," *Journal of Clinical Psychology*, 23 (1967); and M. Manosevitz, "Early Sexual Behavior in Adult Homosexual and Heterosexual Males," *Journal of Abnormal Psychology*, 76 (1970). On the matter of parental influence see M. A. Lewis and L. F. Schoenfeldt, "Developmental-Interest Factors Associated with Homosexuality," *Journal of Consulting and Clinical Psychology*, 41 (1973); and especially H. Siegelman, "Parental Background of Male Homosexuals and Heterosexuals," *Archives of Sexual Behavior*, 3 (1974).

8. Freud himself acknowledged in a footnote the possiblity that this Caterina was a servant, referring to the fact that this was the conclusion of at least one of Leonardo's biographers. Nevertheless, with no evidence to support him, he chose to believe Caterina was Leonardo's mother. For the first direct criticism of Freud on this point, see Maclagan, "Leonardo in the Consulting Room." For Leonardo's other references to Caterina see Edward MacCurdy, ed., *The Notebooks of Leonardo da Vinci* (New York: Braziller, 1958), pp. 62, 1129, 1157.

9. Kurt Eissler, in his *Leonardo da Vinci*, cited above, would take issue with this matter of irrelevance. To Eissler, Freud can have it both ways: if this Caterina was Leonardo's mother, Freud's analysis is correct; however, if she was his servant, Freud's analysis is *still* correct since then *"we are entitled to assume* that she was selected from among the applicants because of her name, and that her name, perhaps also her appearance and age, and her function in the household served to render her a maternal substitute" (p. 92; italics added). There is, of course, no evidence for *any* of this. But more importantly, as we shall discuss later at some length, this trick of using psychoanalytic theory to make any eventuality fit a preordained thesis—of theoretically rendering that thesis immune to disproof—is one of the central logical failings of the psychoanalytic method.

10. David Hackett Fischer calls this problem the "fallacy of the negative proof." It is, as he notes, always worth keeping in mind the elementary fact that "not knowing that a thing exists is different from knowing that it does not exist." *Historians' Fallacies: Toward a Logic of Historical Thought* (New York: Harper, 1970), pp. 47–48.

11. MacCurdy, *Notebooks of Leonardo*, pp. 13–14.

12. See Meyer Schapiro's typically masterful essay, "Leonardo and Freud: An Art-Historical Study," *Journal of the History of Ideas*, XVII (1956).

13. In the 1923 edition of his book Freud inserted a footnote acknowledging the earlier dating of the cartoon, but saying nothing about the smile; rather, in that footnote he pursued other matters pertaining to the positioning of the two female figures.

14. Schapiro, "Leonardo and Freud," esp. pp. 161–64.

15. Ibid., p. 163.

16. Many of these parallels are mentioned in Lichtenberg, "Freud's Leonardo"; other parallels, although not seen as such by the author, can be found in Jones, *Life and Work,* esp. vol. II, part 3.

17. George A. Lindbeck, "Erikson's Young Man Luther: A Historical and Theological Reappraisal," *Soundings,* 52 (1973): 215.

18. Roland H. Bainton, "Psychiatry and History: An Examination of Erikson's 'Young Man Luther,'" *Religion in Life,* 40 (1971); and Heinrich Bornkamm, "Luther and His Father: Observations on Erik H. Erikson's *Young Man Luther,*" in *Childhood and Selfhood: Essays on Tradition, Religion, and Modernity in the Psychology of Erik H. Erikson,* ed. Peter Homans (Lewisburg: Bucknell University Press, 1978). In addition, see Lewis W. Spitz, "Psychohistory and History: The Case of Young Man Luther," *Soundings,* 52 (1973).

19. It should be noted that of all the variants on Freudian analysis Klein's is among the lowest in repute, not only among psychologists in general but among psychoanalysts as well. This is largely because it makes the most of the least verifiable aspects of Freud's work (e.g., the death instinct and the insistence that the superego develops in earliest infancy).

20. See the review by Lewis Perry in *History and Theory,* XVI (1977), esp. p. 185. An important lesson in restraint to the psychohistorian eager to find psychoanalytic grist in medical histories is provided in Edwin A. Weinstein, "Woodrow Wilson's Neurological Illness," *Journal of American History,* 57 (1970).

21. Rogin at one point applies the work of John Bowlby on separation anxiety to Jackson—but Bowlby's concern is with *maternal* deprivation, whereas Jackson's infancy was marked by the absence of his *father.* For this and other pertinent criticisms, see William Gilmore, "The Individual and the Group in Psychohistory: Rogin's *Fathers and Children* and the Problem of Jackson's Health," *The Psychohistory Review,* VI (1977–78).

22. Fischer, *Historians' Fallacies,* p. 109.

23. Walter C. Langer, *The Mind of Adolf Hitler: The Secret Wartime Report* (London: Secker & Warburg, 1973), p. 186; Robert G. L. Waite, "Adolf Hitler's Anti-Semitism: A Study in History and Psychoanalysis," in

The Psychoanalytic Interpretation in History, ed., Benjamin B. Wolman (New York: Basic Books, 1971), p. 203; italics added. Cf. Waite's more complete treatment, *The Psychopathic God, Adolf Hitler* (New York: Basic Books, 1976), and Rudolph Binion, *Hitler Among the Germans* (New York: Elsevier, 1976), esp. pp. 132-33.

24. Sigmund Freud, "Psycho-analytic Notes on an Autobiographical Account of a Case of Paranoia (Dementia Paranoides)," in *Standard Edition*, ed. Strachey, vol. 12, p. 63. Despite its prominence in his theory of paranoia, Freud never developed very fully his ideas on projection; see Ernest Jones, *Life and Work*, vol. II, pp. 270-72.

25. In addition to the studies cited in Chapter 4 on the etiology of paranoia, see W. D. Wells and R. L. Goldstein, "Sears' Study of Projection: Replication and Critique," *Journal of Social Psychology*, 64 (1964).

26. See Schapiro. "Leonardo and Freud," p. 175.

27. See the review by Garry Wills, "Uncle Thomas's Cabin," *The New York Review of Books* (April 18, 1974), pp. 26-28.

Chapter Two

1. K. R. Eissler, *Leonardo da Vinci: Psychoanalytic Notes on The Enigma* (New York: International Universities Press, 1961), p. 293; cf. the same author's *Talent and Genius: The Fictitious Case of Tausk Contra Freud* (New York: Quadrangle, 1971), chap. VII.

2. Ortega y Gasset, "In Search of Goethe from Within," in *The Dehumanization of Art* (New York: Doubleday, 1948), p. 144; discussed in Eissler, *Leonardo*, pp. 290-95.

3. For a discussion of therapists in Ethiopia, Borneo, and elsewhere (including the example of Digat Anak Kutak) see E. Fuller Torrey, *The Mind Game: Witchdoctors and Psychiatrists* (New York: Emerson Hall, 1972). Torrey is a psychiatrist with the National Institute of Mental Health.

4. Freud, "New Introductory Lectures on Psychoanalysis" (1933), in *Standard Edition*, ed. Strachey, vol. 22, p. 152.

5. Freud, "The Interpretation of Dreams" (1900) in *Standard Edition*, ed. Strachey, vol. 5, p. 384.

6. See, for instance, J. Marmor, "Validation of Psychoanalytic Techniques," *Journal of the American Psychoanalytic Association*, 3 (1955); and P. F. D. Seitz, "The Consensus Problem in Psychoanalytic Research," in

Methods of Research in Psychotherapy, eds. L. A. Gottschalk and A. H. Auerbach (New York: Appleton-Century-Crofts, 1966).

7. Freud, "An Outline of Psychoanalysis" (1940) in *Standard Edition*, ed. Strachey, vol. 23, p. 197; E. Glover, "Research Methods in Psychoanalysis," *International Journal of Psychoanalysis*, 33 (1952): 403.

8. P. Knapp et. al, "Suitability for Psychoanalysis: A Review of 100 Supervised Analytic Cases," *Psychoanalytic Quarterly*, 29 (1960): 463. Among many larger surveys of this sort, see W. Weintraub, "A Survey of Patients in Classical Psychoanalysis: Some Vital Statistics," *Journal of Nervous and Mental Disease*, 146 (1968); S. Kadushin, *Why People Go To Psychiatrists* (New York: Atherton, 1969); and D. A. Hamburg, ed., *Report of ad hoc Committee on Central Fact-gathering Data* (New York: American Psychoanalytic Association, 1967). Among the specific figures in these reports are some showing that a third of surveyed patients derive much or all of their income from inheritance or investment, that the percentage of them holding at *least* an undergraduate degree is ten times that of the population at large, and that well over half of them are Jewish.

9. H. Klein, "A Study of Changes Occurring in Patients During and After Psychoanalytic Treatment," in *Current Approaches to Psychoanalysis*, eds. P. Hoch and J. Zubin (New York: Grune & Stratton, 1960); cf. Kadushin, *Why People Go To Psychiatrists*.

10. See S. L. Weiss, "Perceived Effectiveness of Psychotherapy: A Function of Suggestion?" *Journal of Consulting and Clinical Psychology*, 39 (1972); and E. J. Langer and R. P. Abelson, "A Patient By Any Other Name . . . : Clinical Group Difference in Labeling Bias," *Journal of Consulting and Clinical Psychology*, 42 (1974).

11. H. Feifel and J. Eells, "Patients and Therapists Assess the Same Psychotherapy," *Journal of Consulting Psychology*, 27 (1963). Among the numerous psychiatric placebo studies, see, for example, P. Lang et. al, "Desensitization, Suggestibility, Pseudo-Therapy," *Journal of Abnormal Psychology*, 70 (1966).

12. Stanley Rachman, *The Effects of Psychotherapy* (Oxford: Pergamon, 1971), p. 46.

13. Hamburg, *Report of the ad hoc Committee*. For discussions of the report see M. Brody, "Prognosis and Results of Psychotherapy," in *Psychosomatic Medicine*, eds. J. Nodine and J. Moyer, (Philadelphia: Lea & Fobiger, 1962); and Rachman, *Effects of Psychotherapy*, chap. 4.

14. Michael Sherwood, *The Logic of Explanation in Psychoanalysis* (New York: Academic, 1969), p. 262.

15. B. Brody, "Freud's Case-Load," *Psychotherapy: Theory, Research, and Practice,* 7 (1970).

16. Seymour Fisher and Roger P. Greenberg, *The Scientific Credibility of Freud's Theories and Therapy* (New York: Basic Books, 1977), pp. 281, 285.

17. See, among numerous studies, J. C. Beck et. al, "Follow-Up Study of Chronic Psychotic Patients 'Treated' by College Case-Aide Volunteers," *American Journal of Psychiatry,* CXX (1963); J. D. Holzberg et. al, "College Students as Companions to the Mentally Ill," in *Emergent Approaches to Mental Health Problems,* eds. E. L. Cowen, E. A. Gardner, and M. Zax (New York: Appleton-Century-Crofts, 1967); and E. G. Poser, "The Effects of Therapists' Training on Group Therapeutic Outcome," *Journal of Consulting Psychology,* XXX (1966).

18. Many of these so-called therapies are mentioned frequently in the popular press. One that is not, "direct" therapy, perhaps deserves more attention—and notoriety. A variation on psychoanalysis for use with psychotic patients, it is described by its developer, J. Rosen, in *Direct Analysis* (New York: Grune & Stratton, 1953) and in A. Scheflen, *A Psychotherapy of Schizophrenia* (Springfield, Ill.: Thomas, 1961). Reference to a similar technique, known informally as "harassment" therapy, and its use in a San Francisco psychiatric ward can be found in D. L. Stannard, "Ideological Conflict on a Psychiatric Ward," *Psychiatry,* 36 (1973).

19. Hans H. Strupp, "Some Comments on the Future of Psychoanalysis," an address reprinted in *Journal of Contemporary Psychotherapy,* 3 (1971).

20. Fisher and Greenberg, *Scientific Credibility,* p. 15.

21. H. J. Eysenck, "The Effects of Psychotherapy: An Evaluation," *Journal of Consulting Psychology,* XVI (1952).

22. N. Sanford, "Psychotherapy," *Annual Review of Psychology,* 4 (1953): 336; quoted in Rachman, *Effects of Psychotherapy,* pp. 14–15.

23. Arthur Janov, *The Anatomy of Mental Illness* (New York: Putnam, 1971), pp. 209–13.

24. See, for example, Walter Kaufmann, "An Anatomy of the Primal Revolution," *Journal of Humanistic Psychology,* 14 (1974).

25. It would not be difficult to compile an entire volume surveying these studies and their various conclusions. Most of them contain serious limitations (such as one that is critical of Eysenck, but that uses as its own sole criterion for evaluation hospital admission rates for *any reason* at all—mental of physical), and the best of them are filled with statistical problems that are still being discussed. Nevertheless, among those that bear citing are the following: C. Schorer et. al, "Improvement Without Treatment," *Diseases of*

the Nervous System, 29 (1968); R. M. Jurjevich, "Changes in Psychiatric Symptoms Without Psychotherapy," in *An Evaluation of the Results of the Psychotherapies,* ed. S. Lesse (Springfield: Thomas, 1968); and, perhaps the most widely cited assessment since Eysenck, A. E. Bergin, "The Evaluation of Therapeutic Outcomes," in *Handbook of Psychotherapy and Behavior Change,* eds. A. E. Bergin and S. Garfield (New York: Wiley, 1970). This last study, though important, should be read with caution, however, as indicated by the critique in Rachman, *Effects of Psychotherapy,* pp. 28–40.

26. Leo Subotnik, "Spontaneous Remission: Fact or Artifact?" *Psychological Bulletin,* 77 (1972): 46; italics added.

27. Fisher and Greenberg, *Scientific Credibility,* p. 341.

28. Ibid., pp. 390, 413. Freud's own doubts about the therapeutic usefulness of psychotherapy are expresed most clearly in "Analysis Terminable and Interminable" (1937), in *Standard Edition,* ed. Strachey, vol. 23, pp. 209–54.

29. Rachman, *Effects of Psychotherapy,* p. 63.

30. H. J. Eysenck, *The Experimental Study of Freudian Theories* (London: Methuen, 1973), pp. 374–75.

31. R. Bruce Sloane, et. al, *Psychotherapy Versus Behavior Therapy* (Cambridge: Harvard University Press, 1975).

32. Freud, "New Introductory Lectures on Psychoanalysis" (1933), in *Standard Edition,* ed. Strachey, vol. 22, p. 152.

33. *Thirty-fourth Annual Report* of the Friends' Asylum [Asylum for the Relief of Persons Deprived of the Use of Their Reason] (Frankford, Pa.: 1851), pp. 14–15. The reports of other asylums during this period are somewhat less reliable and were criticized for exaggeration by Pliny Earle in a famous piece, *The Curability of Insanity* (Utica, N. Y.: Ellis H. Roberts, 1877). However, more recent study and analysis of Earle's statistics have shown *his* conclusions to be questionable; a recovery rate of roughly 50% at the Worcester Hospital, for example, now seems accurate and typical. That is somewhat better than the rate achieved by modern psychoanalysts dealing *only* with carefully screened neurotics, when premature termination without success is considered as therapeutic failure. For a reconsideration of Earle's figures, see J. S. Bockoven, "Moral Treatment in American Psychiatry," *Journal of Nervous and Mental Disease,* CXXIV (1956): 167–94 and 292–321. Also see Barbara G. Rosenkrantz and Maris A. Vinovskis, "The Invisible Lunatics: Old Age and Insanity in Mid-Nineteenth Century Massachusetts" in *Aging and the Elderly,* ed. Stuart Spicker (New York: Humanities Press, 1978). Rosenkrantz and Vinovskis also have forthcoming work relevant to these matters.

34. Rachman, *Effects of Psychotherapy*, p. 5.

35. D. L. Rosenhan, "On Being Sane in Insane Places," *Science*, 179 (January 1973). It is worth noting further that when the study procedure was reversed and psychiatric staff were informed that a fake patient would soon be admitted to their facility, the staff members independently identified various patients as the fake—even though none had in fact been admitted!

36. Sidney Hook, "Science and Mythology in Psychoanalysis," in *Psychoanalysis, Scientific Method, and Philosophy*, ed. Sidney Hook (New York: New York Univeristy Press, 1959), p. 219.

Chapter Three

1. Bernard Bailyn, in *Philosophy and History: A Symposium*, ed. Sidney Hook (New York: New York University Press, 1963), p. 93.

2. Quoted in "Freud and Literature," in Lionel Trilling, *The Liberal Imagination* (Garden City, N.Y.: Doubleday, 1950), p. 32.

3. Ernest Jones, *Papers on Psycho-Analysis*, 4th ed. (Baltimore: William Wood, 1938), p. 2.

4. For a discussion of Mesmer and other precursors of Freud, see Henri F. Ellenberger, *The Discovery of the Unconscious: The History and Evolution of Dynamic Psychiatry* (New York: Basic Books, 1970); and the frankly combative Thomas Szasz, *The Myth of Psychotherapy* (New York: Doubleday, 1978), chaps. 4–6. Szasz also, it should be noted, has some insightful things to say about Freud's persistent literalizing of figurative terminology—above and beyond the matter of the unconscious.

5. Gilbert Ryle, *The Concept of Mind* (New York: Barnes & Noble, 1949).

6. Ibid., p. 17.

7. Alan R. White, *The Philosophy of Mind* (New York: Random House, 1967), p. 45.

8. C. S. Chihara and J. A. Fodor, "Operationalism and Ordinary Language: A Critique of Wittgenstein," *American Philosophical Quarterly*, 2 (1965).

9. Rudolf Carnap, "Psychology in Physical Language," in *Logical Positivism*, ed. A. J. Ayer (New York: Free Press, 1959), p. 174.

10. J. J. C. Smart, "Sensations and Brain Processes," *Philosophical Review*, 68 (1959); revised and reprinted in *The Philosophy of Mind*, ed. V. C. Chappell (Englewood Cliffs, N.J.: Prentice-Hall, 1962).

11. Sigmund Freud, "Analysis of a Phobia in a Five-Year-Old Boy," in

Standard Edition of the Complete Psychological Works of Sigmund Freud,
ed. James Strachey (London: Hogarth Press, 1955), vol. 10, pp. 5–149.

12. Edward Glover, *On the Early Development of Mind* (New York: International Universities Press, 1956), p. 76.

13. Freud, "Analysis of a Phobia in a Five-Year-Old Boy," p. 111.

14. Ibid., pp. 139–40.

15. Ibid., p. 132.

16. H. Stuart Hughes, *History as Art and as Science* (New York: Harper, 1964), p. 47; cf. Hans Meyerhoff, "On Psychoanalysis and History," *Psychoanalysis and the Psychoanalytic Review,* 49 (1962).

17. Freud, "Analysis of a Phobia in a Five-Year-Old Boy," p. 104.

18. See S. H. Flowerman, "Psychoanalytic Theory and Science," *American Journal of Psychotherapy,* 8 (1954).

19. Freud, "Analysis of a Phobia in a Five-Year-Old Boy," p. 104.

20. Joseph Wolpe and Stanley Rachman, "Psychoanalytic 'Evidence': A Critique Based on Freud's Case of Little Hans," *Journal of Nervous and Mental Disease,* 131 (1960).

21. William P. Alston, "Logical Status of Psychoanalytic Theories," *The Encyclopedia of Philosophy* (New York: Macmillan, 1967), vol. 6, p. 513.

22. On the importance of this dichotomy and its apparent universality see the discussion in Jack Goody, *Death, Property and the Ancestors: A Study of the Mortuary Customs of the Lodagaa of West Africa* (Stanford, Calif.: Stanford University Press, 1962), chap. 2. For an insightful discussion of more specific similarities between psychoanalysis and traditional West African thought regarding the unconscious, see Robin Horton, "Destiny and the Unconscious in West Africa," *Africa,* 31 (1961).

23. Bertrand Russell, *Human Knowledge: Its Scope and Limits* (New York: Simon and Schuster, 1948), p. 482.

24. For particularly incisive discussions of these questions, see John Wisdom, *Other Minds* (Oxford: Blackwell & Mott, 1952), esp. pp. 220–35; and Paul Ziff, "About Behaviorism," *Analysis,* 18 (1958).

25. See, for example, T. R. Miles's use of the principle in *Eliminating the Unconscious: A Behaviorist View of Psychoanalysis* (Oxford: Pergamon, 1966), pp. 36–37, 76–84; cf., for a more philosophical argument, Smart, "Sensations and Brain Processes."

26. Ernest Nagel, "Methodological Issues in Psychoanalytic Theory," in *Psychoanalysis, Scientific Method, and Philosophy,* ed. Sidney Hook (New York: New York University Press, 1959), p. 40.

27. Karl R. Popper, *Conjectures and Refutations: The Growth of Scientific Knowledge* (New York: Harper, 1968), p. 37.

28. Bruce Mazlish, *In Search of Nixon: A Psychohistorical Inquiry* (New York: Basic Books, 1972); Walter C. Langer, *The Mind of Adolf Hitler: The Secret Wartime Report* (New York: Basic Books, 1972); Robert G. L. Waite, *The Psychopathic God, Adolf Hitler* (New York: Basic Books, 1976); Geoffrey Gorer, "Themes in Japanese Culture," in *Personal Character and Cultural Milieu*, ed. D. G. Haring (Syracuse, N.Y.: Syracuse University Press, 1949); and Weston La Barre, "Some Observations on Character Structure in the Orient: The Japanese," *Psychiatry*, 8 (1945).

29. Fawn M. Brodie, *Thomas Jefferson: An Intimate History* (New York: Norton, 1974); Geza Roheim, "The Study of Character Development and the Ontogenetic Theory of Culture," in *Essays Presented to C. G. Seligman*, ed. E. E. Evans-Pritchard (London: Routledge & Kegan Paul, 1934); Owen Berkley-Hill, "The Anal Erotic Factor in the Religion, Philosophy and Character of the Hindus," *International Journal of Psychoanalysis*, 2 (1921).

30. Anal-erotic character traits were Freud's initial insights into the theory of psychosexual character development. See his "Character and Anal Erotism," in *Standard Edition*, ed. Strachey, vol. 9, pp. 167–77.

31. Jones, *Papers on Psycho-Analysis*, pp. 547–53.

32. Mazlish, *In Search of Nixon*, p. 146. Italics added.

33. K. R. Eissler, *Leonardo da Vinci: Psychoanalytic Notes on the Enigma* (New York: International Universities Press, 1961); Jay Gonen, *A Psychohistory of Zionism* (New York: Meridian, 1975), p. 204.

34. Erik H. Erikson, *Childhood and Society* (New York: Norton, 1950), esp. chaps. 7 and 8; Michael Kammen, *People of Paradox* (New York: Knopf, 1972).

35. See Jacques Barzun, *Clio and the Doctors: Psycho-history, Quantohistory and History* (Chicago: University of Chicago Press, 1974), pp. 84, 54.

36. Popper, *Conjectures and Refutations*, p. 37.

37. Edgar A. Levenson, *The Fallacy of Understanding: An Inquiry in the Changing Structure of Psychoanalysis* (New York: Basic Books, 1972), p. 73.

38. David Hackett Fischer, *Historians' Fallacies: Toward a Logic of Historical Thought* (New York: Harper, 1970), pp. 166–67.

39. Murray G. Murphey, "An Approach to the Historical Study of National Character," in *Context and Meaning in Cultural Anthropology*, ed. Melford E. Spiro (New York: The Free Press, 1965). I have treated this study at somewhat greater length elsewhere; see David E. Stannard, "American Historians and the Idea of National Character: Some Problems and Prospects," *American Quarterly*, 23 (1971).

40. Popper, *Conjectures and Refutations*, p. 35.

41. Gorer, "Themes in Japanese Culture," p. 273.

42. Ibid., p. 274.

43. Edward Norbeck and Margaret Norbeck, "Child Training in a Japanese Fishing Community"; Betty B. Lanham, "Aspects of Child Care in Japan: Preliminary Report"; and D. G. Haring, "Japanese National Character: Cultural Anthropology, Psychoanalysis, and History"; all in *Personal Character and Cultural Milieu*, ed. Haring, 3rd ed. (Syracuse, N.Y.: Syracuse University Press, 1956). See also F. N. Kerlinger, "Behavior and Personality in Japan: A Critique of Three Studies of Japanese Personality," *Social Forces*, 31 (1953). In fairness to Gorer, it should be pointed out that his was but one of a series of psychoanalytically informed wartime analyses of the Japanese, virtually all of which shared the same mistaken assumptions.

44. John W. M. Whiting and Irvin L. Child, *Child Training and Personality: A Cross-Cultural Survey* (New Haven: Yale University Press, 1953), p. 74.

45. Robert Coles, *The Mind's Fate: Ways of Seeing Psychiatry and Psychoanalysis* (Boston: Little, Brown, 1975), pp. 201–202.

46. Barzun, *Clio and the Doctors*, p. 51.

47. Roland H. Bainton, "Psychiatry and History: An Examination of Erikson's 'Young Man Luther,'" *Religion in Life*, 40 (1971): 463.

48. David Donald, *Lincoln Reconsidered* (New York: Knopf, 1956), pp. 19–36. See the critique by Robert Skotheim in *Journal of Southern History*, 25 (1959): 256–65. Donald's argument, it is only just to note, was unique in little more than its false tone of methodological preciseness; in its general thrust—that reformist activity was socially aberrant and psychologically traceable to status loss—the argument was quite conventional in the 1950s. See, perhaps the classic statement of this view, Richard Hofstadter, *The Age of Reform* (New York: Knopf, 1955) and Norman Pollack, "Hofstadter on Populism," *Journal of Southern History*, 26 (1960).

49. Raymond Sobel, "What Went Right? The Natural History of the Early Traumatized," in *Interpersonal Explorations in Psychoanalysis: New Directions in Theory and Practice*, ed. Earl G. Witenberg (New York: Basic Books, 1973).

Chapter Four

1. Sigmund Freud, "An Outline of Psychoanalysis," in *Standard Edition of the Complete Psychological Works of Sigmund Freud*, ed. James Strachey (London: The Hogarth Press, 1964), vol. 23, pp. 192–93.

2. Karl R. Popper, *Conjectures and Refutations: The Growth of Scientific Knowledge* (New York: Harper, 1961), p. 38, fn. 3; Robert K. Merton, *Social Theory and Social Structure*, Enlarged Edition (New York: The Free Press, 1968), p. 477.

3. E.g., Paul Kline, *Fact and Fantasy in Freudian Theory* (London: Methuen, 1972). I should perhaps note here that I have chosen not to review psychoanalytic theory regarding female sexuality because this subject has received so much critical attention of late that to pursue it here would be truly to beat a very dead horse. Nonetheless, it is worth pointing out at least in passing that on the matter of the Freudian concept of "penis envy" there has been but *one* serious study *ever* conducted that claims to show support for the concept, and that study—based on dream interpretations—has been shown to be so riddled with logical flaws, pro-Freudian bias, and male conceit that its best use today is as a lesson in how not to conduct research. The study is Calvin Hall and Robert L. Van de Castle, "An Empirical Investigation of the Castration Complex in Dreams," *Journal of Personality*, 33 (1965); see also the critical discussion in Hans J. Eysenck and Glenn D. Wilson, *The Experimental Study of Freudian Theories* (London: Methuen, 1973), pp. 166–67.

4. Freud, "Introductory Lectures on Psycho-analysis," in *Standard Edition*, ed. Strachey (1963), vol. 16, p. 337.

5. Ibid., vol. 15, p. 207.

6. R. R. Sears, *Survey of Objective Studies of Psychoanalytic Concepts* (New York: Social Science Research Council, 1943) p. 136.

7. See, for example, R. Stagner and N. Drought, "Measuring Children's Attitudes Toward Their Parents," *Journal of Educational Psychology*, 26 (1935); and L. Stott, "Adolescents' Dislikes Regarding Parental Behavior and Their Significance," *Journal of Genetic Psychology*, 57 (1940).

8. Calvin Hall, "Strangers in Dreams: An Empirical Confirmation of the Oedipus Complex," *Journal of Personality*, 31 (1963).

9. Stanley M. Friedman, "An Empirical Study of the Castration and Oedipus Complexes," *Genetic Psychology Monographs*, 46 (1952).

10. Ibid., p. 113.

11. R. B. Ammons and H. S. Ammons, "Parental Preferences in Young Children's Doll-Play Interviews," *Journal of Abnormal and Social Psychology*, 44 (1949).

12. J. Kagan and J. Lemkin, "The Child's Differential Perception of Parental Attributes," *Journal of Abnormal and Social Psychology*, 61 (1960).

13. Seymour Fisher and Roger P. Greenberg, *The Scientific Credibility of Freud's Theories and Therapy* (New York: Basic Books, 1977) p. 182.

14. See, for example, Geza Roheim, "The Anthropological Evidence and the Oedipus Complex," *Psychoanalytic Quarterly*, 21 (1952); and J. W. M. Whiting et. al, "The Function of Male Initiation Ceremonies at Puberty," in E. E. Maccoby et. al, *Readings in Social Psychology* (New York: Holt, Rinehart & Winston, 1958).

15. A number of well-known "post-Freudian" adjustments have, of course, been made. Perhaps the most famous are those of Karen Horney and Erich Fromm which rely heavily on specific cultural situations. See Horney's *New Ways in Psychoanalysis* (New York: Norton, 1939), chap. 4; and Fromm's "The Oedipus Complex and the Oedipus Myth," in *The Family: Its Function and Destiny*, ed. R. N. Anshen (New York: Harper, 1948). But see also Arnold W. Green's early, though still acute, critique of these writers for their sociological naïveté in "Sociological Analysis of Horney and Fromm," *American Journal of Sociology*, 51 (1946). A more recent and very perceptive treatment is Anne Parsons, "Is the Oedipus Complex Universal? The Jones-Malinowski Debate Revisited and a South Italian 'Nuclear Complex,'" in *Man and His Culture: Psychoanalytic Anthropology after 'Totem and Taboo'*, ed. Warner Muensterberger (New York: Taplinger, 1969).

16. The two important early studies here, also mentioned in Kline, *Fact and Fantasy in Freudian Theory*, are John Dollard et. al, *Frustration and Aggression* (New Haven: Yale University Press, 1939); and N. E. Miller and R. Bugelski, "Minor Studies of Aggression: The Influence of Frustrations Imposed by the In-Group on Attitudes Expressed Towards Out-Groups," *Journal of Psychology*, 34 (1948).

17. Leo Postman, et. al, "Is There a Mechanism of Perceptual Defense?" *Journal of Abnormal and Social Psychology*, 48 (1953); Gerald S. Blum, "Perceptual Defense Revisited," *Journal of Abnormal and Social Psychology*, 51 (1955). These works discuss the first of the two methods mentioned. A fairly well-known example of the second technique is I. M. Rosenstock, "Perceptual Aspects of Repression," *Journal of Abnormal and Social Psychology*, 46 (1951).

18. David S. Holmes, "Investigations of Repression: Differential Recall of Material Experimentally or Naturally Associated with Ego Threat," *Psychological Bulletin*, 81 (1974), 649.

19. Freud, "On the History of the Psycho-analytic Movement," in *Standard Edition*, ed. Strachey (1957), vol. 14, p. 16.

20. Holmes, "Investigations of Repression," 651.

21. On the relative unimportance of post-genital syndromes and on the

lack of any objective verification of their existence, see Kline, *Fact and Fantasy in Freudian Theory*, pp. 11, 28–30, 44, 92–94.

22. Freud, "Introductory Lectures on Psycho-analysis," in *Standard Edition*, ed. Strachey (1961), vol. 15, p. 208.

23. Frieda Goldman, "Breastfeeding and Character Formation," *Journal of Personality*, 17 (1948–49).

24. Charles A. Barnes, "A Statistical Study of the Freudian Theory of Levels of Psychosexual Development," *Genetic Psychology Monographs*, 45 (1952).

25. A. Lazare et. al, "Oral, Obsessive and Hysterical Personality Patterns: An Investigation of Psychoanalytic Concepts by Means of Factor Analysis," *Archives of Genetic Psychiatry*, 14 (1966). See also the follow-up on this study, "Oral, Obsessive and Hysterical Personality Patterns: Replication of Factor Analysis in an Independent Sample," *Journal of Psychiatric Research*, 7 (1970).

26. Halla Beloff, "The Structure and Origin of the Anal Character," *Genetic Psychology Monographs*, 55 (1957).

27. Paul Kline, "The Anal Character: A Cross-Cultural Study in Ghana," *British Journal of Social and Clinical Psychology*, 8 (1969); cf. Paul Kline, "Obsessional Traits, Obsessional Symptoms and Anal Erotism," *British Journal of Medical Psychology*, 41 (1968)—*and* the critique in Eysenck and Wilson, *The Experimental Study of Freudian Theories*, pp. 95–98.

28. Lillian Cukier Robbins, "The Accuracy of Parental Recall of Aspects of Child Development and of Child Rearing Practices," *Journal of Abnormal and Social Psychology*, 66 (1963).

29. The study showing limited positive correlation is Frieda Goldman-Eisler, "The Problem of 'Orality' and of its Origin in Early Childhood," *Journal of Mental Science*, 97 (1951). The number of contradictory studies is too large to enumerate here, but many of them are mentioned in the following: Kline, *Fact and Fantasy in Freudian Theory*, chap. 5; Harold Orlansky, "Infant Care and Personality" [a now almost classic work], *Psychological Bulletin*, 46 (1949); and N. O'Connor and C. M. Franks, "Childhood Upbringing and Other Environmental Factors," in *Handbook of Abnormal Psychology*, ed. H. J. Eysenck (New York: Basic Books, 1961). Also, on the Goldman-Eisler study itself, see the comments in Eysenck and Wilson, *Experimental Study of Freudian Theories*, pp. 61–64.

30. For reviews of such studies see Kline, *Fact and Fantasy in Freudian Theory*; Orlansky, "Infant Care and Personality"; O'Connor and Franks, "Childhood Upbringing and Other Environmental Factors"; and especially

B. M. Caldwell, "The Effects of Infant Care," in *Review of Child Development Research,* eds. M. L. and L. W. Hoffman (New York: Russell Sage Foundation, 1964), vol. 1.

31. M. I. Hernstein, "Behavioral Correlates of Breast-Bottle Regimes Under Varying Parent-Infant Relationships," *Monographs of the Society for Research in Child Development,* 28 (1963).

32. Jerrold M. Pollak, "Obsessive-Compulsive Personality: A Review," *Psychological Bulletin,* 86 (1979), 228. On the latter point, cf. A. T. Carr, "Compulsive Neurosis: A Review of the Literature," *Psychological Bulletin,* 81 (1974).

33. Kline, *Fact and Fantasy in Freudian Theory,* p. 94; Anthony F. C. Wallace, *Culture and Personality* (New York: Random House, 1968), p. 116.

34. Michael Scriven, "The Experimental Investigation of Psychoanalysis," in *Psychoanalysis, Scientific Method, and Philosophy,* ed. Sidney Hook (New York: New York University Press, 1959), p. 226.

35. Jerome Kagan et. al, *Infancy: Its Place in Human Development* (Cambridge, Mass.: Harvard University Press, 1978), p. 60.

36. For a lucid, if brief, discussion of the close relationship between Erikson's evolving politics and his changing psychological ideas, see Frederick Crews, "American Prophet," *The New York Review of Books,* 22 (October 16, 1975), pp. 9–15.

37. See Kagan et. al, *Infancy,* esp. pp. 164–65; and Jerome Kagan, *The Growth of the Child: Reflections on Human Development* (New York: Norton, 1978).

38. O. W. Hill, "Child Bereavement and Adult Psychiatric Disturbance," *Journal of Psychosomatic Research,* 16 (1972). An excellent example of the kind of *empirical* research that has been done on the relationship between childhood experiences and adult personality is Jerome Kagan and Howard A. Moss, *Birth to Maturity: A Study in Psychological Development* (New York: Wiley, 1962). See also H. E. Jones et. al, "A Progress Report on Growth Studies at the University of California," *Vita Humana,* 3 (1959). The fact that both of these very extensive studies (each a thirty-year-long developmental study) show little personality correlation between childhood and adulthood—although no effort was made to test the specific validity of psychoanalytic theory—should be of major consequence to psychological theory. Indeed, these and other similar reports are now being reflected in the new work by Kagan that has already been cited.

39. Richard Hofstadter, *The Paranoid Style in American Politics and Other Essays* (New York: Knopf, 1965), p. 5; cf. David Brion Davis, *The*

Slave Power Conspiracy and the Paranoid Style (Baton Rouge: Louisiana State University Press, 1969), pp. 3–7.

40. See, for instance, Robert Brandfon, "Specific Purposes and the General Past: Slaves and Slavery," *Journal of Interdisciplinary History*, 3 (1972): 351–56; and William W. Freehling, "Paranoia and American History," *The New York Review of Books*, 17 (September 23, 1971): 36–37, and an exchange of letters between Davis and Freehling, *The New York Review of Books*, 17 (December 2, 1971): 37–38.

41. Bruce Mazlish, *In Search of Nixon: A Psychohistorical Inquiry* (New York: Basic Books, 1972), pp. 84–85.

42. Freud, "Psycho-analytic Notes on an Autobiographical Account of a Case of Paranoia (Dementia Paranoides)," in *Standard Edition*, ed. Strachey (1958), vol. 12, p. 63. (Italics and caps in original.)

43. P. G. Daston, "Perception of Homosexual Words in Paranoid Schizophrenia," *Perception and Motor Skills*, 6 (1956).

44. H. S. Zamansky, "An Investigation of the Psychoanalytic Theory of Paranoid Delusions," *Journal of Personality*, 26 (1956).

45. Ibid., p. 424.

46. Kline, *Fact and Fantasy in Freudian Theory*, p. 275.

47. See, for example, R. Rossi et. al, "The Problem of the Relationship Between Homosexuality and Schizophrenia," *Archives of Sexual Behavior*, 1 (1971).

48. Paul Ricoeur, *Freudian Philosophy: An Essay in Interpretation* (New Haven: Yale University Press, 1970), pp. 344–75; Christopher Lasch, *Haven in a Heartless World: The Family Besieged* (New York: Basic Books, 1977), p. 200, fn. 22; Heinz Hartmann, "Psychoanalysis as a Scientific Theory," in *Psychoanalysis, Scientific Method and Philosophy*, ed. Sidney Hook (New York: New York University Press, 1959), p. 21—cited in Ricoeur; R. D. Laing, "The Study of Family and Social Contexts in Relation to 'Schizophrenia,'" in Laing, *The Politics of the Family and Other Essays* (New York: Pantheon, 1969), p. 44. For discussion of Ricoeur's recommendations, see E. Slater, "Freud: A Philosophical Assessment," *British Journal of Psychiatry*, 120 (1972), 455–457.

Chapter Five

1. John Demos, *A Little Commonwealth: Family Life in Plymouth Colony* (New York: Oxford University Press, 1970), pp. 49–51.

2. Among the more recent such experiments, see E. Hull et. al, "Population Density and Social, Territorial, and Physiological Measures in the Gerbil," *Journal of Comparative and Physiological Psychology,* 84 (1973); Hull et. al, "Effects of Crowding and Intermittent Isolation on Gerbils," *Physiology and Behavior,* 13 (1974); and T. F. Pettijohn and B. M. Barkes, "The Influence of Living Area Space on Behavior in the Mongolian Gerbil," *Journal of Genetic Psychology,* 100 (1979). Cf. J. L. Freedman, *Crowding and Behavior* (San Francisco: Freeman, 1975) and D. Stokols, "The Experience of Crowding in Primary and Secondary Environments," *Environment and Behavior,* 5 (1973)—both of which show that among human populations definitions of space are highly relative and that responses to perceived crowding are dependent upon a wide variety of personal and social variables.

3. Demos, *A Little Commonwealth,* pp. 27, 29; italics added.

4. Ibid., p. 47.

5. D. W. Robertson, Jr., *Chaucer's London* (New York: Wiley, 1968), pp. 5, 11; J. H. van den Berg, *The Changing Nature of Man* (New York: Norton, 1961); Bernard G. Rosenthal, *The Images of Man* (New York: Basic Books, 1971); Philippe Ariès, *Centuries of Childhood: A Social History of Family Life* (New York: Random House, 1962), p. 103. For somewhat more cautious criticism of psychohistory from this perspective, see Dietrich Orlow, "The Significance of Time and Place in Psychohistory," *Journal of Interdisciplinary History,* 5 (1974).

6. Erik H. Erikson, *Young Man Luther: A Study in Psychoanalysis and History* (New York: Norton, 1958), p. 257.

7. David Hackett Fischer, *Historians' Fallacies: Toward a Logic of Historical Thought* (New York: Harper, 1970), p. 49.

8. Hans Jonas, "Change and Permanence: On the Possibility of Understanding History," *Social Research,* 38 (1971): 500–501.

9. Jack W. Meiland, *Scepticism and Historical Knowledge* (New York: Random House, 1965), p. 192.

10. Daniel Cappon, *Technology and Perception* (Springfield, Ill.: Thomas, 1971), p. 38.

11. H. A. Murray, "Toward a Classification of Interactions," in *Toward a General Theory of Action,* eds. Talcott Parsons and E. A. Shils (Cambridge, Mass.: Harvard University Press, 1951), p. 446.

12. Henry James, *The Portrait of a Lady* (Boston: Houghton Mifflin, 1963), p. 7 [from James' 1908 preface to the New York edition of his works].

13. W. H. R. Rivers, "Introduction and Vision" in *Report of the Cambridge Anthropological Expedition to the Torres Straits,* ed. A. C. Haddon

(Cambridge, Eng.: Cambridge University Press, 1901), vol. II; L. Levy-Bruhl, *How Natives Think* [orig. pub. 1910] (London: Allen & Unwin, 1926), p. 43.

14. D. O. Hebb, *Organization of Behavior* (New York: Wiley, 1949); and Homer G. Barnett, *Innovation: The Basis of Cultural Change* (New York: McGraw-Hill, 1953). It is true, of course, that Edward Sapir and Benjamin Whorf, among others, had earlier argued the position that perception is influenced by cognition, which is itself influenced by language. The term perception in these studies was used, however, in more of a metaphorical sense than that employed here, and the connection was considerably more speculative. See R. W. Brown and E. H. Lenneberg, "A Study in Language and Cognition," *Journal of Abnormal and Social Psychology*, 49 (1954), for some penetrating remarks on these early language and perception studies, including the classic example of the various Eskimo terms for snow. On the other hand, for a considerably more sophisticated presentation of the argument that language influences our awareness of reality (including a critique of the Whorf hypothesis) see Joseph Church, *Language and the Discovery of Reality* (New York: Random House, 1961).

15. Anthony F. C. Wallace, *Culture and Personality* (New York: Random House, 1968), p. 122.

16. In R. Redfield et. al, *Aspects of Primitive Art* (New York: Museum of Primitive Art, 1959), p. 56.

17. Hans H. Toch and Richard Schulte, "Readiness to Perceive Violence as a Result of Police Training," *British Journal of Psychology*, 52 (1961); reprinted in *Social Perception*, eds. Toch and Clay Smith (Princeton, N. J.: Van Nostrand, 1968).

18. R. L. Gregory and J. G. Wallace, *Recovery from Early Blindness: A Case Study*, Monograph No. 2 (1963) of the Experimental Psychology Society, Cambridge, England. Reprinted in *Perception: Selected Readings in Science and Phenomenology*, ed. Paul Tibbetts (Chicago: Quadrangle Books, 1969), p. 368.

19. Roy G. D'Andrade, "Cultural Constructions of Reality," paper read at 1971 National Institute of Mental Health Conference in Palo Alto and published in Laura Nader and Thomas W. Maretzki, eds., *Cultural Illness and Health: Essays in Human Adaptation* (Washington: American Anthropological Association, 1973). I am grateful to Professor D'Andrade for sending me a copy of his original manuscript, from which this quotation is taken.

20. For convenient summaries and examples of some such studies, see Toch and Smith, *Social Perception;* W. N. Dember, *The Psychology of Per-*

ception (New York: Holt, 1960); M. D. Vernon, *The Psychology of Perception* (London: Penguin, 1962); and M. D. Vernon, *Experiments in Visual Perception* (London: Penguin, 1968), esp. pp. 333–417.

21. John R. Platt, *Perception and Change* (Ann Arbor: University of Michigan Press, 1970), pp. 44–45.

22. Stephen C. Pepper, "A Dynamic View of Perception," *Philosophy and Phenomenological Research*, 32 (1971): 45, 44.

23. It should not be overlooked that these problems exist not only for the historian but for any social scientist studying or trying to understand others. Historians, however, are more seriously affected, since they cannot directly question their subjects on matters unrevealed by existing data. For one good example of the kind of work that is being done in the social sciences in closely related areas, see the work on the relationship between culture and cognition in Michael Cole et. al, *The Cultural Context of Learning and Thinking* (New York: Basic Books, 1971).

24. Marshall H. Segall, Donald T. Campbell, and Melville J. Herskovits, *The Influence of Culture on Visual Perception* (Indianapolis, Ind.: Bobbs-Merrill, 1966), p. vi.

25. Ibid., p. 84.

26. Ibid., pp. 88–89; italics in original.

27. Ibid., p. 97.

28. Ibid., pp. 213–14; italics added. Although this study remains probably the most extensive field investigation to date, a good bit of subsequent research has sometimes merely confirmed Segal et. al, but much of it has also fruitfully extended the lines of inquiry. See, for example: G. Jahoda, "Geometric Illusions and Environment: A Study of Ghana," *British Journal of Psychology*, 57 (1966); G. Jahoda and B. Stacey, "Susceptibility to Geometrical Optical Illusions According to Culture and Professional Training," *Perception and Psychophysics*, 7 (1970); J. W. Berry, "Ecology, Perceptual Development and the Müller-Lyer Illusion," *British Journal of Psychology*, 59 (1968); J. W. Berry, "Müller-Lyer Susceptibility: Culture, Ecology or Race?" *International Journal of Psychology*, 6 (1971); J. B. Deregowski, "Pictorial Recognition in Subjects from a Relatively Pictureless Environment," *African Social Research*, 5 (1968); and J. B. Deregowski, "Difficulties in Pictorial Depth Perception in Africa," *British Journal of Psychology*, 59 (1968).

29. George S. Klein, *Perception, Motives, and Personality* (New York: Knopf, 1970), p. 4.

30. Thomas S. Kuhn, *The Structure of Scientific Revolutions*, 2nd ed. (Chicago: University of Chicago Press, 1970), p. 113.

31. John W. Atkinson makes this point rather lightheartedly in "The Achievement Motive and Recall of Interrupted and Completed Tasks," in *Studies in Motivation*, ed. David C. McClelland (New York: Appleton-Century-Crofts, 1955). "The achievement motive is viewed as a latent characteristic of personality which is manifested in behavior only when engaged or supported by appropriate environmental cues. . . . A hungry man is more likely to reach for, pick up, and chew an object on a table at which he is sitting if the object happens to be a sandwich than if it happens to be an ashtray." (pp. 501–502).

32. An exception is Gustav Ichheiser's provocative and suggestive chapter, "Social Perception and Moral Judgment," in his *Appearances and Realities* (San Francisco: Jossey-Bass, 1970), pp. 152–67.

33. Klein, *Perception, Motives and Personality*, p. 144; italics in original.

34. I have confined myself here to discussion of substantive confrontation with the solipsistic dilemma of cultural relativism. On a philosophic level the matter is cogently analyzed in Bernard Williams, "The Truth in Relativism," *Proceedings of the Aristotelian Society*, 75 (1974–75).

35. For Schutz's important thinking on this and related matters, see his *Collected Papers, I: The Problem of Social Reality* (The Hague: Martinus Nijhoff, 1971), esp. pp. 7–27.

36. Clifford Geertz, "The Struggle for the Real," in Geertz, *Islam Observed: Religious Development in Morocco and Indonesia* (Chicago: University of Chicago Press, 1971), p. 99.

37. The writing on this subject is enormous in quantity, but for a good introduction see J. W. Berry and P. R. Dasen, eds., *Culture and Cognition: Readings in Cross-Cultural Psychology* (London: Methuen, 1974).

38. Walter B. Cannon, "'Voodoo' Death," *American Anthropologist*, 44 (1942). Cf. the subsequent comments of the following: Curt P. Richter, "On the Phenomenon of Sudden Death in Animals and Man," *Psychosomatic Medicine*, 19 (1957); David Lester, "Voodoo Death: Some New Thoughts on an Old Phenomenon," *American Anthropologist*, 74 (1972); and Barbara W. Lex, "Voodoo Death: New Thoughts on an Old Explanation," *American Anthropologist*, 76 (1974).

39. Claude Lévi-Strauss, *Structural Anthropology* (New York: Basic Books, 1963), chap. 9.

40. These are, of course, widely discussed matters. Some writings worth attention that are concerned with the specific phenomena mentioned are the following: T. Gladwin, "Culture and Logical Process," in *Explorations in Cultural Anthropology: Essays in Honor of George Peter Murdock*, ed. W. H. Goodenough (New York: McGraw-Hill, 1964); Dorothy Lee, *Freedom*

and Culture (Englewood Cliffs, N.J.: Prentice-Hall, 1959); Patricia Marks Greenfield and Jerome S. Bruner, "Culture and Cognitive Growth," in *Handbook of Socialization Theory and Research,* ed. David A. Goslin (Chicago: Rand-McNally, 1969); Peter Lawrence, *Road Belong Cargo* (Manchester, Eng.: Manchester University Press, 1964); Dorothy Lee, "Being and Value in a Primitive Culture," *Journal of Philosophy,* 13 (1949); Paul Bohannan, "Concepts of Time Among the Tiv of Nigeria," *Southwestern Journal of Anthropology,* 9 (1953); Clifford Geertz, *Person, Time, and Conduct in Bali* (New Haven: Yale University Southeast Asia Studies, Cultural Report Series No. 14, 1966); Bert Kaplan and Dale Johnson, "The Social Meaning of Navaho Psychopathology and Psychotherapy," in *Magic, Faith, and Healing,* ed. Ari Kiev (New York: Free Press, 1964).

41. Philippe Ariès, *Centuries of Childhood* and *L'Homme devant la mort* (Paris: Editions du Seuil, 1978); Carolly Erickson, *The Medieval Vision: Essays in History and Perception* (New York: Oxford University Press, 1976); D. W. Robertson, *A Preface to Chaucer: Studies in Medieval Perception* (Princeton, N.J.: Princeton University Press, 1962); William J. Brandt, *The Shape of Medieval History: Studies in Modes of Perception* (New Haven: Yale University Press, 1966); Thomas S. Kuhn, *The Copernican Revolution* (Cambridge, Mass.: Harvard University Press, 1957); Alexandre Koyré, *From the Closed World to the Infinite Universe* (Baltimore: Johns Hopkins University Press, 1957); Fernand Braudel, *Capitalism and Material Life, 1400-1800* (New York: Harper, 1973); Colin Morris, *The Discovery of the Individual, 1050-1200* (New York: Harper, 1972); Peter Burke, *The Renaissance Sense of the Past* (New York: St. Martin's, 1970); Michel Foucault, *Madness and Civilization* (New York: Pantheon, 1965), *The Birth of the Clinic* (New York: Pantheon, 1973), *Discipline and Punish: The Birth of the Prison* (New York: Pantheon, 1977), *The History of Sexuality, Volume I: An Introduction* (New York: Pantheon, 1978); Keith Thomas, *Religion and the Decline of Magic: Studies in Popular Beliefs in Sixteenth and Seventeenth Century England* (London: Weidenfeld and Nicolson, 1971); Lawrence Stone, *The Family, Sex and Marriage in England, 1500-1800* (New York: Harper, 1977); Maria W. Piers, *Infanticide* (New York: Norton, 1978); Norbert Elias, *The Civilizing Process* (New York: Urizen, 1977). See also the forthcoming *Essay in the History of Bourgeois Perception* by Donald M. Lowe.

42. van den Berg, *Changing Nature of Man,* pp. 7-8.

43. On a theoretical level, some of the most suggestive anthropological work in this area remains the discussion of the concepts of "emic" and "etic"—borrowed from the linguistic distinction between phonemics and

phonetics. See K. L. Pike, *Language in Relation to a Unified Theory of the Structure of Human Behavior* (The Hague: Mouton, 1966); D. French, "The Relationship of Anthropology to Studies in Perception and Cognition," in *Psychology: A Study of a Science,* vol. 6, ed. S. Koch (New York: McGraw-Hill, 1963); and W. C. Sturtevant, "Studies in Ethnoscience," in *Transcultural Studies in Cognition,* a special publication of *American Anthropologist,* 66 (1964). Cf. Erving Goffman's important discussion of "primary frameworks" in *Frame Analysis: An Essay on the Organization of Experience* (Cambridge: Harvard University Press, 1974), pp. 21–39.

44. Edgar A. Levenson, *The Fallacy of Understanding: An Inquiry into the Changing Structure of Psychoanalysis* (New York: Basic Books, 1972), p. 111. The references to Erikson are on pp. 96–99 and concern his "reanalysis" of the case of Dora.

Chapter Six

1. A note of caution is necessary here, though it does not deserve elaboration in the text. In an effort to make a silk purse out of a sow's ear (or its equivalent in logical discourse) some friends of psychoanalysis make the intriguing claim that since psychoanalytic theory is so logically flawed it is *immune* to experimental disconfirmation. It then follows, so it is suggested, that either all experimental disconfirmations are invalid or, if they are accepted, that the logical soundness of the theory is thus established. [For a brief allusion to this sort of thinking, see Marie Jahoda, *Freud and the Dilemmas of Psychology* (New York: Basic Books, 1977), pp. 16–17.] This logical naïveté is typical of psychoanalytic thought. First, as we have seen, much of psychoanalytic theory *is* metaphysical (the life and death instincts and the like) and thus untestable, requiring that it be accepted or rejected on faith—like a belief in the Holy Ghost or in transubstantiation. And, like these other alleged phenomena, such aspects of psychoanalytic theory are simply ruled out of scientific consideration. Other matters that are affected by the problem of irrefutability only through timely appeals to the so-called defense mechanisms *are* testable (despite the continuing illogic of the proposition) because even psychoanalysis posits the existence of normality. That is, while in an individual case (the limit, for obvious reasons, which the psychoanalyst wishes to explore) it can always be said that apparent disconfirmation results from the operation of a defense mechanism, in large-scale studies the fact that concepts of normality exist (e. g., that the normal shape of the Oedipus complex is antipathy for the father and attraction to the mother) does permit successful experimentation. What such studies have

most often found, as we have seen, is that no correlation of *any* sort exists. Further, the really critical experimental failure of psychoanalytic theory involves the lack of evidence for postulated *causal* factors, even if the alleged phenomena themselves are spuriously shown to exist; and here the escape clause of irrefutability cannot salvage the theory.

2. For a recent survey of these studies and insightful comments, see Jerome Kagan et. al, *Infancy: Its Place in Human Development* (Cambridge, Mass.: Harvard University Press, 1978), esp. pp. 113–65.

3. P. B. Medawar, "Victims of Psychiatry," *The New York Review of Books*, 21 (January 23, 1975).

4. Lionel Trilling, *Freud and the Crisis of Our Culture* (Boston: Beacon Press, 1955), p. 12.

5. George Hakewill, *An Apologie of the Power and Providence of God in the Government of the World* [orig. pub. 1627] (London, 1635), p. 1.

6. C. P. Snow, "Preface" to Carl Bode, *The Half-World of American Culture* (Carbondale, Ill.: Southern Illinois University Press, 1965), p. viii.

7. Sigmund Freud, *The Future of an Illusion* (New York: Anchor-Doubleday, 1964), pp. 48–51. This can perhaps *begin* to explain (though I venture it only as a suspicion) the paradox of so many tough-talking, self-styled radicals uncritically accepting psychoanalytic ideas with their often politically reactionary consequences. The recent work of Christopher Lasch is a prominent example: compare Lasch's comment that his approach to the past "insists on the historical importance of human actions, and . . . sees history not as an abstract social 'process' but as the product of concrete struggles for power"—an approach that rejects the "mystification of social science" and its alleged claim "that society runs according to laws of its own"—with his starry-eyed acceptance of all manner of unverified, mystifying, and deterministic psychoanalytic ideas. Christopher Lasch, *Haven in a Heartless World: The Family Besieged* (New York: Basic Books, 1977), pp. xv, 200; and *The Culture of Narcissism: American Life in an Age of Diminishing Expectations* (New York: Norton, 1978), *passim*.

8. For some lively discussion of Velikovsky, von Däniken, and other latter-day scientific "paradoxers," see Carl Sagan, *Broca's Brain: Reflections on the Romance of Science* (New York: Random House, 1979), pp. 43–136.

9. Ralph Waldo Emerson, "Historic Notes of Life and Letters in New England," *The Complete Works of Ralph Waldo Emerson*, ed. Edward Waldo Emerson (Cambridge, Mass.: Riverside Press, 1904), vol. 10, pp. 337–39.

10. Erik H. Erikson, *Dimensions of a New Identity* (New York: Norton, (1974), p. 12.

Index

abolitionists, 78–79
Adler, Alfred, 73–74
Alston, William P., 63
Ammons, R. B. and H. S., 171 n11
anal-erotic hypothesis, 67–69, 75, 96–100, 101, 106, 107
Ariés, Philippe, 122, 141, 144
Atkinson, John W., 179 n31

Bailyn, Bernard, 53
Bainton, Roland, 24, 78, 81
Barkes, B. M., 176 n2
Barnes, Charles A., 98–99
Barnett, Homer G., 177 n14
Barzun, Jacques, xiii, 77–78, 81, 168 n35
Beck, J. C., 165 n17
behaviorism, 57–66
Beloff, Halla, 99
Bergin, A. E., 166 n25
Berkley-Hill, Owen, 68
Berry, J. W., 178 n28, 179 n37
Bieber, L., 160 n7

Blum, Gerald S., 95
Bockoven, J. S., 166 n33
body-mind problem, 55–58, 64–66
Bohannan, Paul, 180 n40
Bonaparte, Marie, 22
Bornkamm, Heinrich, 24
Brandfon, Robert, 175 n40
Brandt, William J., 141
Braudel, Fernand, 141
Brodie, Fawn, xi, 28–29, 68
Brody, B., 165 n15
Brody, M., 164 n13
Brown, R. W., 177 n14
Bruner, Jerome S., 180 n40
Bugelski, R., 172 n16
Burke, Peter, 142

Caldwell, B. M., 174 n30
Campbell, Donald T., 134–38
Cannon, Walter B., 140
Cappon, Daniel, 176 n10
Carnap, Rudolf, 58

Carr, A. T., 174 n32
Chesterton, G. K., 70
Chihara, C. S., 167 n8
Child, Irvin L., 76
Church, Joseph, 177 n14
Cole, Michael, 178 n23
Coles, Robert, xx, 77, 81, 159 n16
Collingwood, R. G., 143
Cowen, E. L., 165 n17
Crews, Frederick, 174 n36
Croce, Benedetto, 123

D'Andrade, Roy G., 129–31, 133, 138
Dasen, P. R., 179 n37
Daston, P. G., 110–13
Davis, David B., 108, 109, 114
Davis, Glenn, 158 n9
DeLuca, J. N., 161 n7
de Mause, Lloyd, xi–xii, xvii
Demos, John, 119–21, 158 n9
denial, 69, 93–94
depression, 33–34, 79
Deregowski, J. B., 178 n28
Digat Anak Kutak, 33–35
displacement, 93–94, 107, 119
Dollard, John, 172 n16
Donald, David, 78–79
Drought, N., 171 n7

Earle, Pliny, 166 n33
Ebel, Henry, xii
Eells, J., 164 n11
ego defense mechanisms, 93–96
Einstein, Albert, 67
Eissler, Kurt R., 13, 22, 70
Elias, Norbert, 142
Ellenberger, Henri F., 167 n4
Emerson, Ralph Waldo, 155
endopsychic view of psychoanalysis, 114–16
Erickson, Carolly, 141
Erikson, Erik H., xi, xvi, xvii, 3, 22–24, 70, 78, 105, 122, 144, 155
Eysenck, Hans J., 42–48

Faulkner, William, 125
Febvre, Lucien, 121
Feifel, H., 164 n11
Fischer, David H., 26, 71, 122
Fisher, Seymour, 40, 42, 46, 91
Flowerman, S. H., 168 n18
Fodor, J. A., 167 n8
Foucault, Michel, 142
Franks, C. M., 173 n29
Freedman, J. L., 176 n2
Freehling, William W., 175 n40
French, D., 181 n43
Freud, Anna, 97
Freud, Sigmund, xv, 3–21, 22, 24, 26, 28
  35, 36, 39, 40, 41, 48, 54, 59–62, 70, 74,
  77, 85–86, 88, 91, 97, 100–101, 105, 109,
  122, 154
Friedman, Stanley M., 90–92
Friedn's Asylum, 49
Fromm, Erich, 105, 172 n15

Gardner, E. A., 165 n17
Geertz, Clifford, 140, 180 n40
Gilmore, William, 159 n15, 162 n21
Gladwin, T., 179 n40
Glover, Edward, 59, 164 n7
Goethe, J. W. von, 33–35, 78
Goffman, Erving, 181 n43
Goldman, Frieda, 98
Goldstein, R. L., 163 n25
Gonen, Jay, 70
Goody, Jack, 168 n22
Gorer, Geoffrey, 74–76
Green, Arnold W., 172 n15
Greenberg, Roger, 40, 42, 46, 91
Greenfield, Patricia M., 180 n40
Gregory, R. L., 128–29, 133

Hakewill, George, 153
Hall, Calvin, 90, 171 n3
Hamburg, D. A., 164 n8
Haring, D. G., 75–76
Hartmann, Heinz, 115
Hebb, D. O., 177 n14
Hemings, Sally, 28–29

Hernstein, M. I., 103-104
Herskovits, Melville, 126, 134-38
Hill, O. W., 174 n38
Himmelfarb, Gertrude, 158 n10
Hitler, Adolf, 27, 29, 77, 109
Hofstadter, Richard, 108, 109, 114, 170 n48
Holmes, David S., 95-96
Holzberg, J. D., 165 n17
homosexuality, 7-9, 14-16, 87, 109-114
Hook, Sidney, 50
Horney, Karen, 36, 105, 172 n15
Horton, Robin, 168 n22
Hughes, H. Stuart, x, 60
Huizinga, Johan, 121, 141
Hull, E., 176 n2

Ichheiser, Gustav, 179 n32
infant experience and adult personality, 87, 100-106, 107-108, 150

Jackson, Andrew, 25-26, 29, 116
Jahoda, G., 178 n28
Jahoda, Marie, 181 n1
James, Henry, 125
Janov, Arthur, 44
Jefferson, Thomas, 28-29, 68
Johnson, Dale, 180 n40
Jonas, Hans, 123
Jones, Ernest, 13, 54, 68-69, 92-93, 96
Jones, H. E., 174 n38
Jordan, Winthrop, 28
Joyce, James, 125
Jung, C. G., 11
Jurjevich, R. M., 166 n25

Kadushin, S., 164 n8
Kagan, Jerome, 105, 171 n12, 174 n37, 174 n38, 182 n2
Kammen, Michael, 70
Kaplan, Bert, 180 n40
Kaufmann, Walter, 165 n24
Kerlinger, F. N., 170 n43
Klein, George S., 137

Klein, H., 164 n9
Klein, Melanie, 25
Kline, Paul, 94, 99, 104
Knapp, P., 164 n8
Kohut, Heinz, 143
Koyré, Alexandre, 141
Krauthammer, Charles, 158 n10
Kuhn, Thomas S., 137, 141, 144

La Barre, Weston, 68
Laing, R. D., 116
Lang, P., 164 n11
Langer, Walter C., 27, 67, 77
Langer, William L., ix-x, 81
Lasch, Christopher, 115, 182 n7
Lawrence, Peter, 180 n40
Lazare, A., 98-99
Lee, Dorothy, 179, 180 n40
Lemkin, J., 171 n12
Lenneberg, E. H., 177 n14
Leonardo da Vinci, Freud on, 3-21, 28, 77, 132
Lester, David, 179 n38
Levenson, Edgar A., 71, 143-44
Lévi-Strauss, Claude, ix, 140
Levy-Bruhl, L., 125, 138
Lewis, M. A., 161 n7
Lex, Barbara W., 179 n38
Lichtenberg, Joseph D., 13
Lindbeck, George A., 162 n17
"Little Hans," 59-62, 85-86
Lowe, Donald M., 180 n41
Luther, Martin, 22-24, 29, 78, 116

MacCurdy, Edward, 18
Maclagan, Eric, 160 n4, 161 n8
Malinowski, Bronislaw, 92-93
Manosevitz, M., 161 n7
Marmor, J., 163 n6
Mazlish, Bruce, 67, 69, 108-109
Medawar, P. B., 150
Meiland, Jack W., 123
Merezhkovsky, D. S., 12
Merton, Robert K., 86
Mesmer, Franz Anton, 54
Meyerhoff, Hans, 60

Miles, T. R., 168 n25
Miller, N. E., 172 n16
Möller, Emil, 160 n6
Morris, Colin, 142
Moss, Howard A., 174 n38
Moyer, J., 164 n13
Murphey, Murray G., 71–73, 75
Murray, H. A., 176 n11

Nagel, Ernest, 67
Nixon, Richard, 27, 67, 69, 70, 109
Nodine, J., 164 n13
Norbeck, E. and M., 170 n43

Oakeshott, Michael, 123
"Ockham's razor," 65–66
O'Connor, N., 173 n29
Oedipus complex, 85–86, 87, 88–93, 106–107
oral-erotic hypothesis, 96–100, 101, 106, 107
Orlansky, Harold, 173 n29
Orlow, Dietrich, 176 n5
Ortega y Gasset, José, 33

paranoia, 27, 87, 88, 108–114
Parsons, Anne, 172 n15
Pepper, Stephen C., 132
perception, 124–38
Perry, Lewis, 162 n20
Pettijohn, T. F., 176 n2
Pfister, Oskar, 11
Piers, Maria W., 142
Pike, K. L., 181 n43
Platt, Gerald M., xvii
Platt, John R., 132
Pollack, Norman, 170 n48
Pollak, Jerrold M., 104
Popper, Karl R., 67, 70, 73, 86
Poser, E. G., 165 n17
Post hoc, ergo propter hoc, 24, 66, 71–73
Postman, Leo, 95
projection, 27, 69, 93–94
Protagoras, 124–25

pseudoscience, 154–55
psychosexual personality syndromes, 87, 96–100

Rachman, Stanley, 38, 47, 49, 61–62, 86
Rapaport, David, 158 n13
reaction-formation, 68–70, 89
refutation, problem of, 66–71, 76, 148–49
relativism, cultural, 121–44, 151
repression, 87, 93–96, 106, 107
Richter, Curt P., 179 n38
Ricoeur, Paul, 114–16
Rivers, W.H.R., 125
Robbins, Lillian C., 173 n28
Robertson, D. W., 121–22, 141
Rogin, Michael P., 25–26
Roheim, Geza, 68, 172 n14
Rosen, J., 165 n18
Rosenhan, D. L., 49
Rosenkrantz, Barbara G., 166 n33
Rosenstock, I. M., 172 n17
Rosenthal, Bernard G., 122
Rossi, R., 175 n47
Russell, Bertrand, 64–65
Ryle, Gilbert, 55

Sagan, Carl, 182 n8
Sapir, Edward, 177 n14
Schapiro, Meyer, 18, 20
Scheflen, A., 165 n18
Schoenfeldt, L. F., 161 n7
Schorer, C., 165 n25
Schulte, Richard, 127–28, 133
Schutz, Alfred, 139
Scriven, Michael, 105
Sears, Robert R., 89–90
Segall, Marshall H., 134–38
Seitz, P.F.D., 163 n6
Shakow, David, 158 n13
Sherwood, Michael, 39–40
Siegelman, H., 161 n7
Slater, E., 175 n48
Sloane, R. Bruce, 166 n31
Smart, J.J.C., 58
Snow, C. P., 153

Sobel, Raymond, 79
Spitz, Lewis W., 162 n17
Spock, Benjamin, 102
"spontaneous remission," 42-46, 47
Stacey, B., 178 n28
Stagner, R., 171 n7
Stannard, David E., 169 n39
Stannard, D. L., 165 n18
Stites, Raymond, 11
Stokols, D., 176 n2
Stone, Lawrence, 142
Stott, L., 171 n7
Strachey, James, 13
Strupp, Hans, 41-42
Sturtevant, W. C., 181 n43
sublimation, 4, 69, 93-94
Subotnik, Leo, 45
Sullivan, Harry S., 105
Szasz, Thomas, 167 n4

therapy, psychoanalytic, 35-50, 148
Thomas, Keith, 142
Toch, Hans H., 127-28, 133
Torrey, E. Fuller, 163 n3
Trilling, Lionel, 152, 167 n2

unconscious, Freudian conception of, 54-58, 76, 87, 107

Van de Castle, Robert L., 171 n3
van den Berg, J. H., 122, 142
Velikovsky, Immanuel, 154
Vernon, M. D., 178 n20
Vinovskis, Maris A., 166 n33
von Däniken, Erich, 155
vulture fantasy (Leonardo), 5-6, 11-14

Waite, Robert G. L., 27, 67
Wallace, Anthony F. C., 104, 126
Wallace, J. G., 128-29, 133
Weinstein, Edwin A., 162 n20
Weinstein, Fred, xvii
Weintraub, W., 164 n8
Weiss, S. L., 164 n10
Wells, W. D., 163 n25
White, Alan R. 55-56
Whiting, John W. M., 76, 172 n14
"wild" psychoanalysis, xvii
Williams, Bernard, 179 n34
Wills, Garry, 29
Wisdom, John, 168 n24
Whorf, Benjamin, 177 n14
Wolpe, Joseph, 61-62, 86

Zamansky, H. S., 110-13
Zax, M., 165 n17
Ziff, Paul, 168 n24